i

May this book be your guide to simplifying organization, enhancing teamwork, and achieving success with ease—both personally and professionally.

Here's to your growth and efficiency!

Table of Contents

Introduction 2

  What You Will Learn in This Book....................................... 2

  How to Use This Book: A Step-by-Step Guide for Beginners......... 3

  Overview of OneDrive and SharePoint: What They Are and Why They Matter 4

    What is OneDrive? 4

    What is SharePoint? 5

Part I: Getting Started with OneDrive 7

Chapter 1: Introduction to OneDrive....................................8

  Key Benefits of OneDrive: 9

  Key Features of OneDrive 9

    1. Cloud Storage... 9

    2. File Syncing.. 10

    3. File Sharing and Collaboration................................. 11

    4. Version History 12

  Benefits of Using OneDrive for File Storage and Collaboration . 13

  Understanding OneDrive's Role in the Microsoft Ecosystem 14

Chapter 2: Setting Up OneDrive................................... 16

  Creating a Microsoft Account 16

    Step-by-Step Instructions:................................. 16

  Signing Up for OneDrive 17

    Step-by-Step Instructions:................................. 17

Downloading and Installing the OneDrive App 18

Step-by-Step Instructions for Desktop (Windows and Mac): 18

Step-by-Step Instructions for Mobile (iOS & Android): 19

Setting Up OneDrive on Your Computer............................. 21

Step-by-Step Instructions for Windows:.......................... 21

Step-by-Step Instructions for macOS: 22

Setting Up OneDrive on Mobile Devices (iOS & Android)........... 22

Step-by-Step Instructions for iOS: 23

Step-by-Step Instructions for Android: 23

Chapter 3: Navigating OneDrive...................................... **24**

Understanding the OneDrive Interface (Web & App) 24

Web Interface (Desktop).. 24

Desktop App (Windows/Mac) 25

Mobile App (iOS & Android) 28

Key Sections of the OneDrive Dashboard............................ 29

Web Interface (Desktop).. 29

Desktop App (Windows/Mac) 30

Mobile App (iOS & Android) 30

Customizing Your OneDrive View...................................... 30

Organizing Files and Folders.. 32

Chapter 4: Uploading and Managing Files **35**

Uploading Files and Folders to OneDrive 35

Web Interface (Desktop).. 35

Desktop App (Windows/Mac) 36

Mobile App (iOS & Android) 37

Organizing Files with Folders and Subfolders 39

Renaming, Moving, and Deleting Files 41

Web Interface (Desktop) 41

Desktop App (Windows/Mac) 43

Mobile App (iOS & Android) 43

Using the OneDrive Recycle Bin 43

Chapter 5: Sharing Files and Folders 46

How to Share Files and Folders in OneDrive 46

Web Interface (Desktop) 46

Desktop App (Windows/Mac) 49

Mobile App (iOS & Android) 51

Setting Permissions: View, Edit, and Collaborate 51

Web Interface (Desktop) 51

Desktop App (Windows/Mac) 53

Mobile App (iOS & Android) 53

Managing Shared Links 54

Sharing with Specific People vs. Public Links 55

Web Interface (Desktop) 55

Desktop App (Windows/Mac) 57

Mobile App (iOS & Android) 58

Chapter 6: Syncing Files with OneDrive 59

Setting Up OneDrive Sync 59

Desktop App (Windows) 59

Mobile App (iOS & Android) 60

Syncing Files for Offline Access..................................... 62

Managing Synced Files on Your Desktop 64

Troubleshooting Syncing Issues 66

Chapter 7: Version History and File Recovery 68

Understanding OneDrive's Version History............................ 68

Restoring Previous Versions of Files 71

Web Interface (Desktop)... 71

Desktop App (Windows) 71

Mobile App (iOS & Android) 72

File Recovery in OneDrive.. 72

Using OneDrive's File Recovery Feature 75

Web Interface (Desktop)... 75

Desktop App (Windows) 75

Chapter 8: Collaboration in OneDrive 77

Collaborating on Documents in Real-Time........................... 77

Web Interface (Desktop)... 77

Desktop App (Windows) 78

Mobile App (iOS & Android) 79

Using Microsoft Office Apps for Co-Authoring...................... 79

Adding Comments and Track Changes................................ 81

Web Interface (Desktop)... 81

Desktop App (Windows) 83

Mobile App (iOS & Android) 84

Notifying Collaborators of Changes 84

    Web Interface (Desktop)...85

    Desktop App (Windows)...85

    Mobile App (iOS & Android) 85

Chapter 9: Advanced OneDrive Features 86

Setting Up Auto-Save and Backup 86

    Web Interface (Desktop)...86

    Desktop App (Windows)...87

    Mobile App (iOS & Android) 87

Managing Storage Space in OneDrive..88

Integrating OneDrive with Microsoft Teams.......................................90

    Web Interface (Desktop)...90

    Desktop App (Windows)...90

    Mobile App (iOS & Android) 92

Using OneDrive for Business (Enterprise Features) 92

Part II: Getting Started with SharePoint................................. 95

Chapter 10: Introduction to SharePoint................................. 96

What is SharePoint? 96

SharePoint vs. OneDrive: Key Differences...97

Types of SharePoint Sites: Team Sites vs. Communication Sites
....98

    Team Sites: 98

    Communication Sites:..99

Understanding SharePoint's Role in Collaboration and
Document Management 100

    Collaboration: 100

    Document Management: 101

Chapter 11: Setting Up SharePoint 102

    1. Creating a SharePoint Account 102

    2. Creating Your First SharePoint Site 103

    3. Choosing Between Team Sites and Communication Sites 108

        Team Sites: 108

        Communication Sites: 108

        Choosing the Right Site: 109

    4. Configuring Your Site's Settings 109

        For Desktop (Web Interface): 109

        For Mobile Devices (iOS/Android): 110

Chapter 12: Navigating SharePoint 111

    1. Exploring the SharePoint Interface 111

        For Desktop (Web Interface): 111

        For Mobile Devices (iOS/Android): 112

    2. Understanding Document Libraries and Lists 112

        Document Libraries: 113

        Lists: 115

    3. Accessing Sites and Libraries 116

    4. Customizing Your SharePoint View 117

        For Desktop (Web Interface): 117

For Mobile Devices (iOS/Android): 117

Chapter 13: Working with Document Libraries **119**

1. Uploading Documents to SharePoint Libraries 119

2. Organizing Files in Libraries with Folders and Metadata..... 122

Using Folders: 122

Using Metadata: 122

3. Checking In/Out Documents in SharePoint 123

4. Managing File Versions in SharePoint Libraries 126

Tips for Managing Document Libraries: 127

Chapter 14: Managing SharePoint Permissions **128**

1. Understanding Permissions and Security in SharePoint 128

Permission Levels: 128

SharePoint Security Groups: 129

2. Setting Permissions for Users and Groups 129

For Desktop (Web Interface): 129

For Mobile Devices (iOS/Android): 130

3. Managing Access to Document Libraries 131

For Desktop (Web Interface): 131

For Mobile Devices (iOS/Android): 133

4. Understanding SharePoint Groups and Roles 133

Creating and Managing SharePoint Groups: 133

Assigning Roles to Groups: 134

Best Practices for Managing Permissions: 134

Chapter 15: Sharing and Collaborating in SharePoint **136**

1. Sharing Documents and Folders in SharePoint 136

For Desktop (Web Interface): 136

For Mobile Devices (iOS/Android): 137

2. Inviting External Users to SharePoint 137

For Desktop (Web Interface): 137

For Mobile Devices (iOS/Android): 138

3. Setting Permissions for Shared Content 138

4. Collaboration Features: Comments, Alerts, and Notifications
.... 140

Comments: 140

Alerts: 141

Notifications: 143

Best Practices for Sharing and Collaborating: 143

Chapter 16: Using SharePoint Lists 144

1. What Are SharePoint Lists? 144

Key Features of SharePoint Lists: 145

2. Creating and Managing Lists in SharePoint 145

For Desktop (Web Interface): 145

Managing Lists: 146

For Mobile Devices (iOS/Android): 146

3. Adding, Editing, and Deleting List Items 146

4. Customizing List Views and Columns 147

Customizing Columns: 147

Customizing Views: 148

For Mobile Devices (iOS/Android): 148

Best Practices for Using SharePoint Lists: 149

Chapter 17: Automating Tasks with Workflows 150

1. Introduction to SharePoint Workflows 150

Why Use Workflows in SharePoint? 150

2. Creating and Managing Basic Workflows 151

For SharePoint Online (using Power Automate): 151

Managing Workflows: 152

3. Automating Processes with Power Automate 152

Advanced Power Automate Scenarios: 152

Using Templates: 153

4. Best Practices for SharePoint Workflows 154

Best Practices: 154

Common Workflow Pitfalls to Avoid: 155

Chapter 18: Advanced SharePoint Features 156

1. Creating Custom SharePoint Forms 156

How to Create Custom Forms in SharePoint: 156

Customizing Forms in Power Apps: 157

2. Integrating SharePoint with Microsoft Teams 158

How to Integrate SharePoint with Microsoft Teams: 158

3. Managing Site Collections 159

How to Manage Site Collections: 159

4. Using Power Apps with SharePoint 160

Integrating Power Apps with SharePoint: 160

Part III: Onedrive and SharePoint Together.............................. **162**

Chapter 19: Onedrive and SharePoint Integration **163**

1. How Onedrive and SharePoint Work Together........................163

Key Differences Between Onedrive and SharePoint:..............163

2. Syncing SharePoint Document Libraries with Onedrive 164

How to Sync SharePoint Document Libraries with Onedrive:
....164

Managing Sync Settings:...165

3. Accessing SharePoint Files via Onedrive 165

How to Access SharePoint Files via Onedrive:.........................166

Accessing Files Without an Internet Connection:....................166

4. Co-authoring Documents Stored in SharePoint Using Onedrive
....166

How to Co-author Documents in SharePoint Using Onedrive:
....167

Chapter 20: Cross-Platform Collaboration **168**

1. Using Onedrive and SharePoint on Desktop, Mobile, and Web
....168

On Desktop:...168

On Mobile:...169

On the Web:...169

2. Collaborating on Files Across Devices 170

Co-Authoring Documents: 170

Accessing Files on Multiple Devices: 170

Document Comments and Feedback:...............................171

3. Using SharePoint and OneDrive Offline 171

Offline Access with OneDrive: 171

Offline Access with SharePoint: 172

Chapter 21: Advanced Collaboration Tools 173

1. Microsoft Teams Integration with SharePoint and OneDrive 173

Using Teams with OneDrive: 173

Using Teams with SharePoint: 174

File Permissions and SharePoint Integration: 174

2. Using Planner and To-Do with SharePoint 174

Using Planner with SharePoint: 175

Using To-Do with SharePoint: 175

3. Real-Time Co-Authoring with Office Apps 175

Co-Authoring in OneDrive: 176

Co-Authoring in SharePoint: 176

4. Using SharePoint and OneDrive for Project Management 176

Project Management with SharePoint: 177

Project Management with OneDrive: 177

Tracking Progress and Team Communication: 177

Part IV: Advanced Tips and Best Practices 179

Chapter 22: Managing Storage and Data 180

1. Monitoring OneDrive and SharePoint Storage Usage 180

Monitoring OneDrive Storage Usage: 180

Monitoring SharePoint Storage Usage: 181

2. Cleaning Up Files and Folders to Save Space 181

Cleaning Up OneDrive: 182

Cleaning Up SharePoint: 182

3. Setting Storage Limits and Quotas in SharePoint 183

Setting SharePoint Site Storage Limits: 183

Quota Management: 183

4. Best Practices for File Organization and Management 184

Best Practices for OneDrive: 184

Best Practices for SharePoint: 184

Chapter 23: Security and Compliance 186

1. Securing Your Files and Documents in OneDrive and
SharePoint 186

OneDrive Security Features: 186

SharePoint Security Features: 187

2. Understanding Encryption and Data Privacy 187

Encryption in OneDrive and SharePoint: 187

Data Privacy Considerations: 188

3. Setting Up Multi-Factor Authentication (MFA) 189

What is MFA?: 189

Setting Up MFA for OneDrive and SharePoint: 189

4. SharePoint's Security and Compliance Features 190

Compliance Center: 190

Data Loss Prevention (DLP) in SharePoint: 190

Retention Policies: 191

Advanced Threat Protection (ATP): 191

Chapter 24: Troubleshooting Common Issues 192

1. Solving Sync Problems in OneDrive 192

Possible Causes of Syncing Issues: 192

Solutions: 193

Other Fixes: 193

2. Dealing with Permission Errors in SharePoint 194

Possible Causes of Permission Issues: 194

Solutions: 194

3. Fixing Common File Upload Problems 195

Possible Causes of Upload Problems: 195

Solutions: 195

4. Resolving Conflicts in Document Libraries 196

Possible Causes of File Conflicts: 196

Solutions: 197

Part V: Real-Life Use Cases and Scenarios 198

Chapter 25: Personal Use of OneDrive and SharePoint 199

1. Using OneDrive for Personal File Storage and Backup 199

Key Features for Personal Use: 199

How to Use OneDrive for Personal File Storage: 200

2. Organizing Photos and Videos in OneDrive 200

Organizing Photos in OneDrive: 201

Using OneDrive's Search Features: 201

3. SharePoint for Personal Projects and Collaboration 202

Using SharePoint for Personal Projects: 202

Collaborating in SharePoint: 202

Benefits of Using OneDrive and SharePoint for Personal Use .203

OneDrive for Personal Use: 203

SharePoint for Personal Use: 204

Chapter 26: Small Business Use.. 205

1. Setting Up OneDrive and SharePoint for Small Teams 205

Getting Started with OneDrive: 205

Setting Up SharePoint: 206

2. Collaborative Document Management for Small Businesses
....207

Collaborating with OneDrive: 207

Collaborating with SharePoint: 207

3. Best Practices for Team Collaboration and File Sharing 208

Best Practices for Using OneDrive and SharePoint: 208

Tips for Secure File Sharing: 209

Chapter 27: Corporate and Enterprise Use 211

1. Enterprise-Level File Management with SharePoint............. 211

Key Features for Enterprise File Management: 211

Document Retention Policies: 212

2. Managing Teams and Permissions in SharePoint for Large
Organizations 212

Organizing Teams and Sites: 212

Managing Permissions: 213

Monitoring and Auditing: 213

3. Enterprise-Level Storage and Security Management 214

Storage Solutions: 214

Security Features: 214

Compliance Management: 215

Index **217**

Introduction

Welcome to **OneDrive & SharePoint Made Easy: A Step-by-Step Guide for Beginners**! Whether you're new to cloud storage or already familiar with the basics, this guide will take you on a journey through two of the most powerful tools in Microsoft's suite: **OneDrive** and **SharePoint**. These tools help you store, organize, share, and collaborate on files seamlessly across multiple devices.

Both **OneDrive** and **SharePoint** play pivotal roles in enhancing productivity, streamlining workflows, and simplifying file management. By the end of this book, you will be proficient in using both tools to manage your documents and collaborate efficiently with others.

You don't need to be a tech expert to get started. This book is designed to be **beginner-friendly**, breaking down each feature step by step and explaining **how** and **why** you would use them.

What You Will Learn in This Book

In this book, you will learn the ins and outs of both **OneDrive** and **SharePoint**, starting from the basics and progressing to more advanced techniques. Here's a preview of what you will master:

- **Setting up OneDrive**: Learn how to create an account, install the OneDrive app, and set it up on your desktop, mobile, and web.
- **Managing Files in OneDrive**: Understand how to upload, organize, and manage files with ease across platforms.
- **Collaborating with Others**: Learn how to share files, co-author documents, and collaborate in real time.
- **Syncing Your Files**: Discover how to sync your files across devices, making sure you always have access to your data.
- **Exploring SharePoint**: Dive into SharePoint's capabilities, including creating sites, managing permissions, and collaborating on a broader scale.
- **Integration between OneDrive and SharePoint**: Understand how these tools work together, enabling efficient cross-platform collaboration.

Additionally, this book will provide tips, tricks, and troubleshooting solutions, so you'll feel confident in tackling any challenges that arise along the way.

How to Use This Book: A Step-by-Step Guide for Beginners

This book is designed to be **easy-to-follow** and **comprehensive** for beginners. Here's how to use it most effectively:

- **Start at the Beginning**: If you're new to OneDrive and SharePoint, begin with the first chapter. We'll take you step-by-step through the basics and guide you through the setup process.

- **Follow the Chapter Breakdown**: Each chapter is divided into smaller, digestible sections. You'll find clear **step-by-step instructions** for each task, with screenshots and visuals where needed to help you along the way.
- **Different Devices, Different Instructions**: We understand that you may use OneDrive and SharePoint on **different devices** (desktop, mobile, or web). To ensure clarity:
  - **Desktop app**: Instructions for Windows and Mac desktop apps will be outlined separately, so you know exactly how to set up and manage files on your computer.
  - **Web interface**: For those who prefer accessing these tools online, we'll walk you through the web-based platforms for both OneDrive and SharePoint.
  - **Mobile app**: You'll also learn how to use OneDrive and SharePoint on your mobile device, allowing you to access and edit your files on the go.
- **Progress at Your Own Pace**: You can follow the chapters in order or skip ahead to the sections that interest you most. Each chapter builds upon the last, so if you're not familiar with a particular feature, feel free to revisit earlier chapters.

Overview of OneDrive and SharePoint: What They Are and Why They Matter

Before diving into the technical details, let's first understand what **OneDrive** and **SharePoint** are, and how they can significantly enhance your productivity and file management.

What is OneDrive?

OneDrive is a **cloud-based storage service** that allows you to store files, photos, documents, and more. It offers **seamless syncing across devices**, so your files are always accessible whether you're working on a computer, tablet, or smartphone. With OneDrive, you can:

- Store files online to free up space on your devices.
- **Sync** files across different devices, ensuring you always have access to the latest version.
- **Share** files and folders easily with others, whether for work or personal use.
- **Collaborate** on documents in real-time using Office apps like Word, Excel, and PowerPoint.

Whether you're working on a single document or managing a huge library of files, OneDrive gives you **secure storage**, **easy sharing**, and **cross-device access**.

What is SharePoint?

SharePoint, on the other hand, is a **web-based collaboration platform** primarily used by businesses and organizations. It allows teams to create **sites**, **manage documents**, and **collaborate on content**. SharePoint helps you:

- Create **team sites** to organize documents, calendars, tasks, and conversations for your team.
- **Share documents** across your organization, ensuring everyone has access to the most up-to-date versions.
- **Customize workflows** to automate processes, such as document approvals or project tracking.

- **Integrate** with Microsoft 365 apps, such as Microsoft Teams, Outlook, and Planner, to create a seamless collaborative experience.

SharePoint is often used by **businesses and enterprises** to manage large volumes of documents and enable team collaboration, but it's also useful for **personal and small team projects**.

By understanding the distinct roles of OneDrive and SharePoint, you will be able to choose the right tool for your specific needs and use them efficiently together to optimize your file management and collaboration workflows.

Part I: Getting Started with OneDrive

Chapter 1: Introduction to OneDrive

Onedrive is a **cloud-based storage service** provided by Microsoft. It allows you to store files, documents, photos, videos, and much more on the cloud, making them accessible from virtually any device. Whether you're working on your computer, smartphone, or online, **OneDrive** ensures that your files are always available and in sync across all platforms.

Cloud storage means that your files are stored on Microsoft's secure servers rather than only on your local devices. This ensures that you can access your documents from anywhere, share them with others, and keep them safe even if something happens to your device.

Key Benefits of OneDrive:

- **Access Anywhere**: Access your files from any device with an internet connection.
- **Automatic Backup**: Your files are stored securely online, protecting them from accidental loss.
- **Collaboration**: Share files and collaborate on documents in real time with others.

What Does OneDrive Offer?

Remote Access

Collaboration

Mobile Access

File Types

Basic Security

Key Features of OneDrive

OneDrive offers several **powerful features** designed to enhance how you store and work with your files. Here's an overview of the key features:

1. Cloud Storage

With OneDrive, you can store **documents, photos, videos, and more** securely in the cloud. You can free up space on your computer or mobile device while keeping all your files easily accessible.

Step-by-Step Instructions for Using Cloud Storage:

- **Desktop App**:
    1. Open the **OneDrive app** on your computer.
    2. Drag files or folders into the OneDrive folder to upload them to the cloud.
    3. Once uploaded, the files will automatically sync across all devices linked to your OneDrive account.
- **Web Interface**:
    1. Go to **OneDrive.com** and sign in with your Microsoft account.
    2. Click on the **"Upload"** button to upload files or folders.
    3. Once uploaded, your files will appear in the OneDrive web interface and sync with your other devices.
- **Mobile App**:
    1. Open the **OneDrive app** on your mobile device.
    2. Tap the **"+"** icon to upload files from your phone.
    3. Your files will sync across devices and be available on the web.

2. File Syncing

OneDrive automatically syncs files across your devices, ensuring you have access to the latest version, no matter which device you use.

Step-by-Step Instructions for Syncing Files:

- **Desktop App**:
  1. Ensure the OneDrive app is running in the background.
  2. Any files or folders you add to the OneDrive folder will automatically sync to the cloud.
  3. If you edit a file on one device, the changes will sync to all other devices with OneDrive installed.
- **Web Interface**:
  1. Files you upload through the web interface will sync to your OneDrive account and be accessible from the desktop or mobile app.
  2. Any updates made to documents through the web interface will sync across your devices.
- **Mobile App**:
  1. Files synced to OneDrive will be available in the mobile app for viewing and editing.
  2. When you update a file, the changes sync to the cloud, making them available on all devices.

3. File Sharing and Collaboration

OneDrive makes it easy to share files with others and collaborate in real-time. You can share a link to a file or folder and grant others permissions to **view**, **edit**, or **comment** on the content.

Step-by-Step Instructions for Sharing Files:

- **Desktop App**:
  1. Right-click on the file or folder you want to share.

2. Select **"Share"** from the menu.
3. Choose whether to send an email invite or create a shareable link.
4. Select permissions (view or edit) and send the invite.

- **Web Interface**:
  1. Click on the file or folder you want to share.
  2. Click the **"Share"** button at the top of the screen.
  3. Choose between sending an email invite or generating a shareable link.
  4. Set permissions (can edit or view) and send the invite.

- **Mobile App**:
  1. Tap the **three dots** next to the file or folder you want to share.
  2. Tap **"Share"**.
  3. Select whether to send an email or generate a link.
  4. Choose the permissions (view or edit) and share the file.

4. Version History

OneDrive allows you to view and restore previous versions of documents. This is particularly useful if you want to track changes or recover content that was accidentally deleted.

Step-by-Step Instructions for Version History:

- **Desktop App**:
  1. Right-click the file you want to check version history for.
  2. Select **"Version History"**.

3. Choose the version you want to view or restore.
- **Web Interface**:
  1. Right-click the file and select **"Version History"**.
  2. Select the version you want to restore.
- **Mobile App**:
  1. Tap on the file to open it.
  2. Tap the **three dots** in the top-right corner and select **"Version History"**.
  3. Choose the version you wish to restore.

Benefits of Using OneDrive for File Storage and Collaboration

OneDrive provides several benefits that make it an excellent choice for personal and professional file storage:

1. Secure Storage

All files stored in OneDrive are backed up in Microsoft's **secure cloud environment**, providing an extra layer of protection for your data. With **encryption** and **multi-factor authentication**, your files are safe from unauthorized access.

2. Easy Collaboration

OneDrive integrates seamlessly with Microsoft 365 applications like **Word, Excel,** and **PowerPoint.** You can **co-author documents**, make edits in real-time, and collaborate with team members, all while ensuring that everyone has the most current version of the file.

3. Cost-Effective

OneDrive offers **free cloud storage** with an initial 5 GB, and you can easily upgrade to additional storage through the **Microsoft 365** subscription, which provides generous storage limits and a range of other useful features.

4. Cross-Platform Accessibility

Whether you're using **Windows**, **macOS**, **Android**, or **iOS**, OneDrive ensures your files are always available across all your devices, without the hassle of transferring files manually.

Understanding OneDrive's Role in the Microsoft Ecosystem

OneDrive is an essential component of the broader **Microsoft ecosystem**, integrating seamlessly with other Microsoft tools and services. Here's a breakdown of how OneDrive fits into the larger Microsoft suite:

1. Integration with Microsoft 365

OneDrive is tightly integrated with **Microsoft 365** apps like **Word**, **Excel**, **PowerPoint**, and **Outlook**. You can open and save documents directly from OneDrive, collaborate with others, and manage your files with ease.

2. Microsoft Teams and SharePoint

OneDrive works hand-in-hand with **Microsoft Teams** and **SharePoint** for collaboration and file sharing. While OneDrive is designed for personal file storage, SharePoint and Teams are better suited for team and project collaboration. You can store documents in SharePoint or Teams and sync them with your personal OneDrive for easy access.

Chapter 2: Setting Up OneDrive

B efore you can start using OneDrive, you'll need a **Microsoft account**. This account serves as your gateway to all of Microsoft's services, including OneDrive.

Creating a Microsoft Account

Step-by-Step Instructions:

- **Desktop (Web Interface)**:
  1. Open your web browser and navigate to the Microsoft Sign-Up Page at account.microsoft.com/account.
  2. Click on **"Create one!"** under the "Sign In" button.
  3. Enter your **email address** (you can use any email address, but a Microsoft email is recommended, e.g., **@outlook.com**).
  4. If you don't have an email yet, you can create a new **Outlook.com** or **Hotmail.com** account during the process.
  5. Follow the prompts to set up your **password** and **security options** (phone number or email for recovery).
  6. Once you've filled out all the required information, click **"Create Account"**.
- **Mobile App (iOS & Android)**:

1. Download and install the **Microsoft Authenticator** app or **OneDrive app** from your app store (App Store for iOS, Google Play for Android).
2. Open the app and tap on **"Sign Up"** or **"Create Account"**.
3. Follow the instructions to enter your **email** and **password**.
4. Verify your account using a **security code** sent to your email or phone.

Signing Up for OneDrive

Once you have a Microsoft account, you can **sign up** for OneDrive. Signing up for OneDrive is essentially linked to your Microsoft account, and you can access OneDrive immediately by logging into it.

Step-by-Step Instructions:

- **Web Interface (Desktop)**:
  1. Open your **browser** and visit **OneDrive.com**.
  2. Click on **"Sign In"** at the top-right corner.
  3. Enter the **Microsoft account** you just created and click **"Next"**.
  4. Enter your **password** and click **"Sign In"**.
  5. Once signed in, OneDrive will automatically be linked to your Microsoft account, and you'll be taken to your OneDrive dashboard where you can upload, manage, and share your files.
- **Desktop App**:

1. Download the **OneDrive app** (discussed in the next section).
2. Open the app and **sign in** with your Microsoft account (email and password).
3. Once signed in, the app will link to your **OneDrive cloud storage**, syncing your files and folders automatically.

- **Mobile App** (iOS & Android):
  1. Download the **OneDrive app** from your respective **App Store**.
  2. Open the app and tap **"Sign In"**.
  3. Enter your **Microsoft account** credentials (email and password).
  4. Once logged in, you'll have access to your cloud storage and can start uploading and managing files.

Downloading and Installing the OneDrive App

To use OneDrive on your desktop or mobile device, you must download the **OneDrive app**. The app helps sync files across devices and access them from anywhere.

Step-by-Step Instructions for Desktop (Windows and Mac):

- **Windows**:
  1. Open the **Microsoft Store** (search for it in the Start Menu).
  2. In the search bar, type **"OneDrive"** and click the **OneDrive app**.
  3. Click on **"Get"** to download and install the app.

4. Once installed, open the app, and follow the prompts to **sign in** with your Microsoft account.
5. The app will create a **OneDrive folder** on your computer where all your synced files will be stored.

- **Mac**:
    1. Go to the **OneDrive Download Page**.
    2. Download the **OneDrive app** for macOS.
    3. Open the downloaded file to start the installation process.
    4. Once installed, open the app and **sign in** using your Microsoft account.
    5. The app will sync files to the **OneDrive folder** on your Mac.

Step-by-Step Instructions for Mobile (iOS & Android):

- **iOS**:
    1. Open the **App Store** on your iPhone or iPad.
    2. Search for **"OneDrive"**.
    3. Tap **"Install"** to download and install the app.
    4. Open the app, and sign in with your **Microsoft account**.
    5. Start uploading, syncing, and managing your files directly from the app.
- **Android**:
    1. Open the **Google Play Store** on your Android phone or tablet.
    2. Search for **"OneDrive"**.
    3. Tap **"Install"** to download and install the app.
    4. Open the app and **sign in** with your Microsoft account.

5. You'll now be able to upload and access files stored in OneDrive.

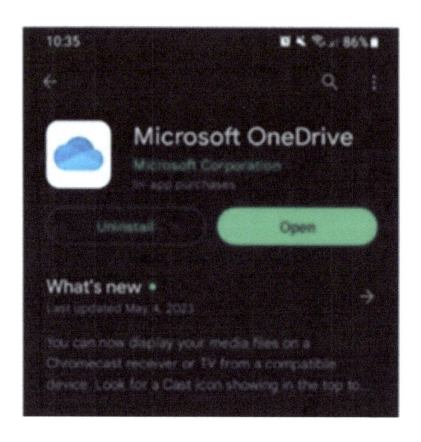

 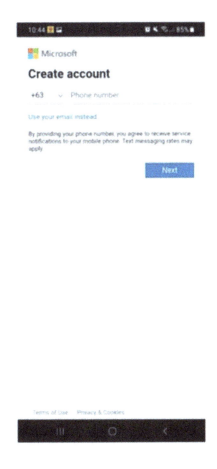

Setting Up OneDrive on Your Computer

Once the **OneDrive app** is installed on your computer, you'll need to configure it to start syncing your files.

Step-by-Step Instructions for Windows:

1. **Open OneDrive**:
   - Find the **OneDrive icon** in your taskbar (it looks like a cloud).

- o If the icon isn't visible, click the **up arrow** to see all running apps.
2. **Sign In**:
   - o If not already signed in, click on the OneDrive icon, then select **"Sign In"**.
   - o Enter your **Microsoft account** credentials (email and password).
3. **Choose Sync Folder**:
   - o After signing in, you'll be asked to choose the **OneDrive folder** where your files will be stored. You can select the default or create a new folder.
4. **Sync Files**:
   - o After setting up, any files you place into the OneDrive folder will automatically sync to the cloud, accessible from all devices linked to the same Microsoft account.

Step-by-Step Instructions for macOS:

1. Open the **OneDrive app** on your Mac.
2. Enter your **Microsoft account** credentials (email and password).
3. Choose a location for your **OneDrive folder** (or accept the default location).
4. OneDrive will automatically sync your files to the cloud.

Setting Up OneDrive on Mobile Devices (iOS & Android)

OneDrive is available as a mobile app for both **iOS** and **Android** devices, making it easy to upload, access, and manage your files on the go.

Step-by-Step Instructions for iOS:

1. Open the **App Store** on your iPhone/iPad and search for "**OneDrive**".
2. Download and install the **OneDrive app**.
3. Open the app and **sign in** with your **Microsoft account**.
4. You can now upload and access your files directly from the app.
5. To **sync files**, simply tap the **"Upload"** button (a plus icon) to add files or folders from your device to the cloud.

Step-by-Step Instructions for Android:

1. Open the **Google Play Store** and search for "**OneDrive**".
2. Download and install the **OneDrive app**.
3. Open the app and **sign in** with your **Microsoft account**.
4. To **upload files**, tap the **"+"** icon to select files from your device.
5. Your files will sync to OneDrive, making them accessible on any device linked to your account.

Chapter 3: Navigating OneDrive

The OneDrive interface may look slightly different depending on the platform you're using, but the core functionality remains the same. Let's walk through how to navigate the interface on the **web**, **desktop app**, and **mobile app**.

Understanding the OneDrive Interface (Web & App)

Web Interface (Desktop)

1. **Login**:
   - Open your web browser and navigate to **onedrive.com**.
   - Sign in using your **Microsoft account** credentials (email and password).
2. **Main Sections**:
   - After logging in, you'll be directed to the **OneDrive dashboard**. The main sections of the web interface include:
     - **Navigation Pane** (left side): Includes access to **"My files"**, **"Shared"**, **"Recycle Bin"**, **"Photos"**, **"Recent"**, and other areas.
     - **Main Area** (center): Displays your **files** and **folders** with their names, modification dates, and sharing statuses.
     - **Top Bar**: Includes buttons for **New**, **Upload**, **Sort**, and options for **Settings** and **Help**.

3. **Key Elements**:
   - **Search Bar**: Located at the top of the page, allowing you to search for files and folders.
   - **Sort Options**: Use the **Sort** dropdown to arrange your files by **name**, **date modified**, or other criteria.

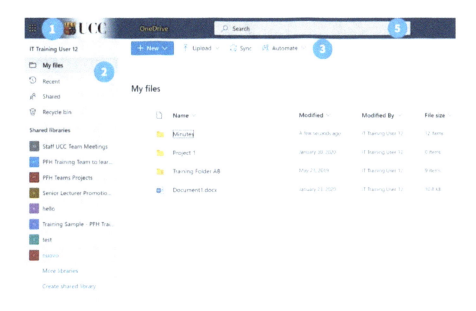

Desktop App (Windows/Mac)

1. **Opening the App**:
   - On Windows, you'll find the **OneDrive icon** in the **taskbar** (bottom-right corner). On macOS, look for the icon in the **menu bar** (top-right corner).

- ○ Clicking on the icon opens the **OneDrive settings** menu, and clicking **"Open OneDrive Folder"** will show your synced files and folders in **File Explorer** (Windows) or **Finder** (Mac).

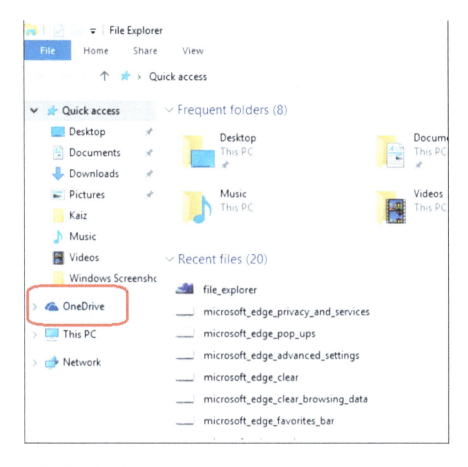

2. **Key Sections**:
   - **OneDrive Folder**: The folder on your computer that syncs with the cloud. Any file you add here is automatically uploaded to OneDrive.
   - **Files and Folders**: You can **drag and drop** files into this folder, and they will sync to the cloud.
   - **Sync Status**: Files that are syncing or have already synced show a **checkmark icon** (Windows) or a **green dot** (Mac).
3. **Navigating**:

- In **File Explorer** or **Finder**, you can **right-click** on files and folders for options like **share**, **move**, and **delete**.

Mobile App (iOS & Android)

1. **Opening the App**:
   - Launch the **OneDrive app** on your **iPhone**, **iPad**, or **Android** device.
2. **Main Sections**:
   - **Home**: Your recent files, files shared with you, and recommended files will appear here.
   - **Files**: Browse through all your files and folders stored in OneDrive.
   - **Search**: Tap the **search bar** to quickly find files by name.
   - **Me**: Access your personal settings, account, and storage information.
3. **Navigation Tips**:
   - Tap and hold on files to see options for **sharing, deleting**, or **moving** them.
   - Use the **bottom menu bar** to switch between **Home, Files, Photos**, and **Shared** views.

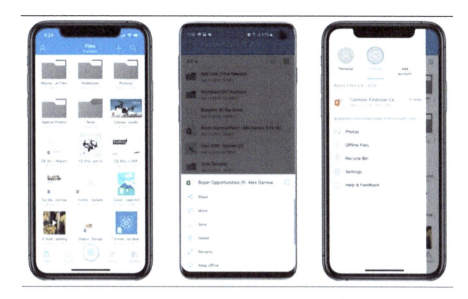

Key Sections of the OneDrive Dashboard

Now that we understand the overall layout of the interface on each platform, let's dive deeper into the key sections you'll frequently use in OneDrive's **Dashboard**.

Web Interface (Desktop)

1. **My Files**: This section displays your files and folders stored in OneDrive. You can access your **documents**, **photos**, and **videos** from here.
2. **Recent**: Displays the files you've recently opened or edited.
3. **Shared**: Files that others have shared with you or files you have shared with others.
4. **Recycle Bin**: Deleted files are stored here temporarily, where you can either restore them or permanently delete them.

5. **Photos**: Displays all images and videos from your OneDrive account.
6. **Personal Vault**: A secure area for sensitive documents that require extra verification for access.

Desktop App (Windows/Mac)

- The desktop app essentially integrates OneDrive into your system's **file explorer** or **Finder**, which makes it easier to access files directly from your computer's native file management system.
- **Cloud Files**: Files stored online only, with a cloud icon.
- **Locally Available Files**: Files stored both on your computer and OneDrive, shown with a **green check**.

Mobile App (iOS & Android)

1. **Home**: The **Home** section on mobile mirrors the dashboard you see in the web and desktop versions, showing recently accessed files and suggested content.
2. **Files**: Direct access to all your files and folders.
3. **Shared**: View files shared with you and files you've shared with others.
4. **Camera Upload**: Enable automatic backup of photos and videos from your mobile device to OneDrive.
5. **Activity**: View recent activity such as edits or shares.

Customizing Your OneDrive View

OneDrive allows you to adjust how you view and interact with your files and folders, making it easier to stay organized.

Web Interface (Desktop)

1. **Change View Type**:
   o Click on the **View** button at the top-right corner of your file list (next to Sort) to toggle between **List** view and **Thumbnail** view.
   o **List View** is perfect for seeing file details such as **date modified**, **size**, and **type**.
   o **Thumbnail View** allows you to see previews of images and documents.
2. **Organize Files**:
   o Click on the **Sort** button at the top to sort by **Name**, **Date Modified**, **Size**, or **Type**.
   o You can also use the **Filter** option to show only certain types of files (e.g., Word documents, photos, etc.).
3. **Change File or Folder Names**:
   o Right-click on any file or folder and select **Rename** to change its name.

Desktop App (Windows/Mac)

1. **View File Status**:
   o The **OneDrive folder** integrates into File Explorer or Finder, and you can **right-click** on files to see **Sync status** (e.g., **green check** means synced, **cloud icon** means only online).
2. **Change Folder Location**:
   o In the **OneDrive settings**, you can **choose folders** to sync or change the location of your OneDrive folder.

Mobile App (iOS & Android)

1. **View Files**:
   o On mobile, swipe through your files in either **grid** or **list** format by selecting the **View** icon at the top of the screen.
2. **Customize Sort**:
   o Tap the **three dots** in the upper-right corner to change how files are sorted. You can organize by **name, size**, or **date modified**.

Organizing Files and Folders

Now that we've covered the basics of navigating the OneDrive interface and customizing your view, let's discuss how to stay organized by creating folders and managing files.

Web Interface (Desktop)

1. **Create a New Folder**:
   o From the **OneDrive dashboard**, click the **"New"** button at the top-left corner.
   o Select **Folder** and enter a name for the folder.

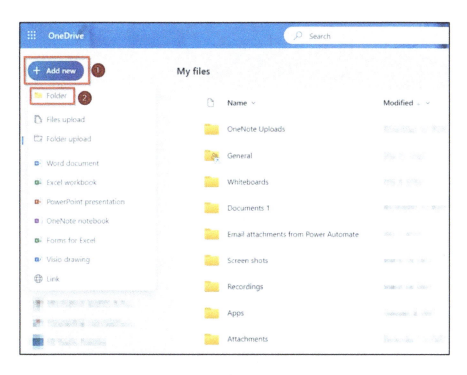

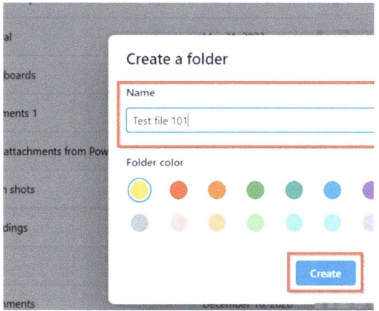

- o Click **Create**.
2. **Move Files**:
   - o To move a file into a folder, simply **drag and drop** it into the folder in your OneDrive dashboard.
3. **Delete Files**:
   - o Right-click on any file or folder and select **Delete** to move it to the **Recycle Bin**.

Desktop App (Windows/Mac)

1. **Create Folders**:
   - o In the **OneDrive folder** on your desktop, **right-click** and select **New Folder**.
   - o Name the folder and press **Enter**.
2. **Organize Files**:
   - o Simply **drag and drop** files and folders into the desired location.

Mobile App (iOS & Android)

1. **Create Folders**:
   - o Open the **OneDrive app** and tap on the **three lines** in the top-left corner to open the **navigation menu**.
   - o Tap on **"New Folder"** and enter the folder name.
   - o Tap **Create** to save the folder.
2. **Move Files**:
   - o Tap and hold a file or folder, select **Move**, and then choose the new location.

Chapter 4: Uploading and Managing Files

Onedrive makes it easy to upload files and folders from your computer or mobile device to the cloud. Below, we'll cover how to do this for the **web**, **desktop app**, and **mobile app**.

Uploading Files and Folders to OneDrive

Web Interface (Desktop)

1. **Uploading Individual Files**:
   - Go to **onedrive.com** and log into your account.
   - In the **My Files** section, click the **"Upload"** button at the top of the page.
   - Select **"Files"** from the dropdown menu.

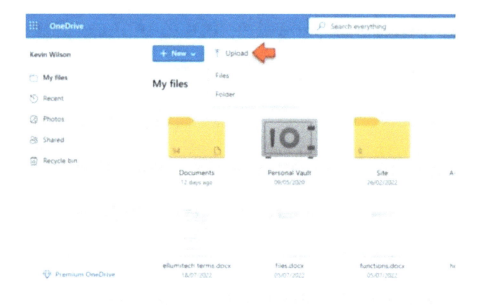

- A file explorer window will pop up. **Select the files** you want to upload, and click **"Open"**.
- The files will begin uploading, and you'll see a progress indicator in the top-right corner.

2. **Uploading Folders**:
   - Click the **"Upload"** button again and select **"Folder"** from the dropdown menu.
   - Choose the folder you want to upload from your computer and click **"Upload"**.
   - The folder, along with all its contents, will be uploaded to OneDrive.

Desktop App (Windows/Mac)

1. **Uploading Files Using File Explorer/Finder**:

- Open the **OneDrive folder** in **File Explorer** (Windows) or **Finder** (Mac).
- Simply **drag and drop** the files or folders you want to upload into the OneDrive folder.
- The files will automatically begin syncing with the cloud. You'll see a **green checkmark** when the upload is complete.

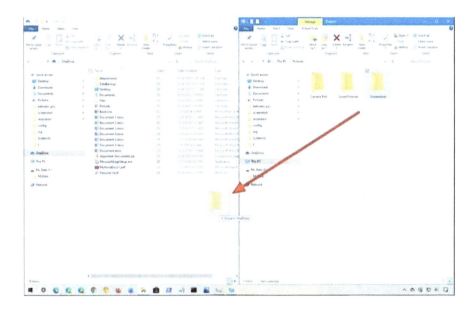

2. **Using the Right-Click Menu**:
   - You can also **right-click** on any file or folder within the OneDrive folder and select **"Move to OneDrive"** (or drag it to the OneDrive folder).
   - This will initiate the upload process.

Mobile App (iOS & Android)

1. **Uploading Individual Files**:

- Open the **OneDrive app** on your mobile device.
- Tap the **"+"** icon (usually at the bottom of the screen).
- Select **"Upload"**, and then choose the **"Files"** option.
- Navigate to the file you want to upload and select it. The file will upload to OneDrive.

2. **Uploading Photos or Videos**:
   - Open the **OneDrive app** and tap the **"+"** icon.
   - Choose **"Upload"** and select **"Photos and Videos"**.
   - Select the images or videos you want to upload from your gallery. They will be uploaded to OneDrive.

3. **Uploading Entire Folders (on Android only)**:
   - To upload a folder, tap the **"+"** icon, select **"Upload"**, then choose **"Folder"**.
   - Navigate to the folder you wish to upload and select it. On iOS, folder uploads are not yet supported.

Organizing Files with Folders and Subfolders

OneDrive helps you stay organized by allowing you to create folders and subfolders. Here's how to organize your files and folders across all platforms.

Web Interface (Desktop)

1. **Creating a New Folder**:
   - In the **My Files** section, click on the **"New"** button on the top-left.
   - Select **"Folder"** from the dropdown menu.
   - A new folder will appear, and you can enter the folder name.
   - Hit **"Enter"** to create the folder.
2. **Creating Subfolders**:
   - Open the folder where you want to create a subfolder.
   - Click on **"New"** and select **"Folder"** again.
   - Name your subfolder and press **Enter**.
3. **Moving Files into Folders**:
   - To move files into a folder, click and **drag** the file over to the target folder, or right-click the file and select **"Move to"**.
   - Select the destination folder or create a new one.
4. **Renaming Files or Folders**:
   - Right-click any file or folder and select **"Rename"**.
   - Type the new name and hit **Enter**.

Desktop App (Windows/Mac)

1. **Creating Folders and Subfolders**:

- Open your **OneDrive folder** in **File Explorer** (Windows) or **Finder** (Mac).
- Right-click anywhere inside the OneDrive folder and choose **"New Folder"**.
- Name the folder and press **Enter**.
- You can create subfolders by following the same steps inside existing folders.

2. **Organizing Files**:
   - Simply **drag and drop** your files into folders or subfolders within the OneDrive folder on your computer.

3. **Renaming Files or Folders**:
   - Right-click the file or folder, and select **"Rename"** from the context menu.
   - Type the new name and hit **Enter**.

Mobile App (iOS & Android)

1. **Creating a New Folder**:
   - Open the **OneDrive app** and tap on the **three dots** (menu) next to your main folder or in an empty space.
   - Tap **"New Folder"**.
   - Name the folder and tap **"Create"**.

2. **Creating Subfolders**:
   - Navigate to a folder and tap the **three dots** icon within it.
   - Select **"New Folder"** to create subfolders.

3. **Organizing Files**:
   - To move files, tap and hold on a file, select **"Move"**, and choose the folder where you want to move the file.

4. **Renaming Files or Folders**:
   - Tap and hold the file or folder, then select **"Rename"** from the menu.
   - Enter the new name and save.

Renaming, Moving, and Deleting Files

Managing files, including renaming, moving, and deleting, is a crucial part of file organization in OneDrive.

Web Interface (Desktop)

1. **Renaming Files or Folders**:
   - Right-click on any file or folder and choose **"Rename"**.
   - Enter a new name and press **Enter**.

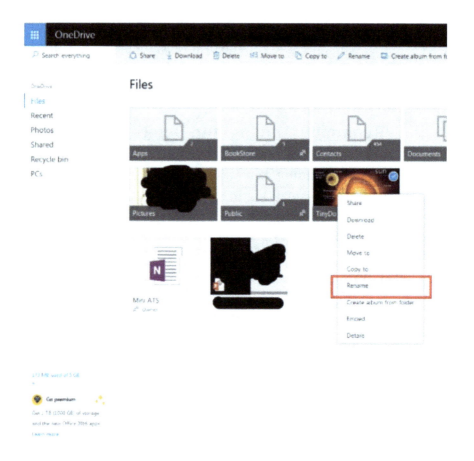

2. **Moving Files or Folders**:
   - Right-click the file/folder and select **"Move to"**.
   - Choose the target folder or create a new folder.
3. **Deleting Files or Folders**:
   - Right-click on a file or folder and select **"Delete"**.
   - Confirm your choice to move the file/folder to the **Recycle Bin**.

Desktop App (Windows/Mac)

1. **Renaming Files or Folders**:
   - In **File Explorer** (Windows) or **Finder** (Mac), right-click on the file/folder and select **"Rename"**.
   - Type the new name and hit **Enter**.
2. **Moving Files or Folders**:
   - Drag and drop files or folders into other folders within the **OneDrive folder**.
3. **Deleting Files or Folders**:
   - Right-click on the file/folder and select **"Delete"** to move it to the **Recycle Bin**.

Mobile App (iOS & Android)

1. **Renaming Files or Folders**:
   - Tap and hold the file or folder you wish to rename.
   - Select **"Rename"** from the menu and enter the new name.
2. **Moving Files or Folders**:
   - Tap and hold the file/folder, select **"Move"**, and choose the destination folder.
3. **Deleting Files or Folders**:
   - Tap and hold on the file/folder and select **"Delete"** to send it to the **Recycle Bin**.

Using the OneDrive Recycle Bin

The **Recycle Bin** in OneDrive is where deleted files go temporarily before being permanently removed. Here's how to manage your deleted items.

Web Interface (Desktop)

1. **Accessing the Recycle Bin**:
   - On the left-hand side of the OneDrive web interface, click on **"Recycle Bin"** under **"My Files"**.
   - Here, you'll see all deleted files and folders.
2. **Restoring Files**:
   - Select the file(s) you want to restore.
   - Click **"Restore"** at the top of the page to recover the file back to its original location.
3. **Permanently Deleting Files**:
   - Select the file(s) you want to delete permanently.
   - Click **"Delete"** at the top to remove it permanently from OneDrive.

Desktop App (Windows/Mac)

- The Recycle Bin can be accessed through the **OneDrive website** since the desktop app only syncs files and doesn't have a local Recycle Bin.

Mobile App (iOS & Android)

1. **Accessing the Recycle Bin**:
   - In the OneDrive app, tap the **"Me"** icon in the bottom-right corner.
   - Select **"Recycle Bin"** to view deleted items.
2. **Restoring Files**:
   - Tap and hold on the deleted file and select **"Restore"** to recover the file.
3. **Permanently Deleting Files**:

- Tap and hold the file, then select **"Delete Permanently"** to remove it completely from OneDrive.

Chapter 5: Sharing Files and Folders

Onedrive provides robust options for sharing files and folders, making it easy to collaborate with others. Whether you are working with colleagues, family, or friends, OneDrive ensures that sharing is safe, secure, and flexible.

How to Share Files and Folders in OneDrive

Sharing files and folders in OneDrive is straightforward. Below are the steps for sharing via the **web, desktop,** and **mobile apps.**

Web Interface (Desktop)

1. **Sharing a File or Folder:**
   o   Go to **onedrive.com** and log in to your account.
   o   Navigate to **My Files** and select the file or folder you want to share.
   o   Right-click the file/folder or click the three-dotted menu next to it and select **"Share".**

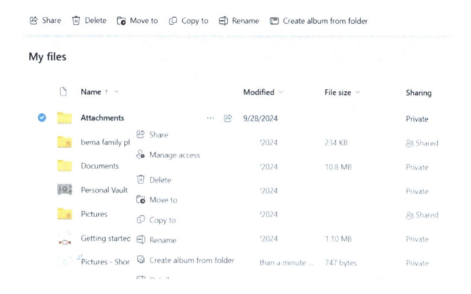

Right-click on the file or folder and select share

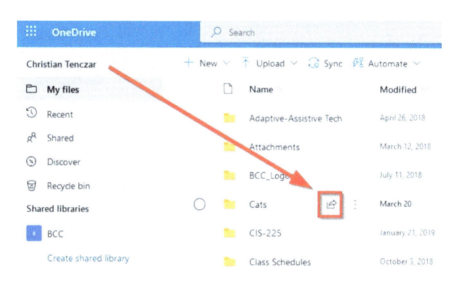

Alternatively, lick on the share icon next to the file or folder

- o   In the sharing window, you'll see a link that you can either **copy** or **send via email** directly from the window.
- o   If you want to adjust settings, click **"Anyone with the link"** (you can change this later), and select whether you want them to **edit** or **view** the file.

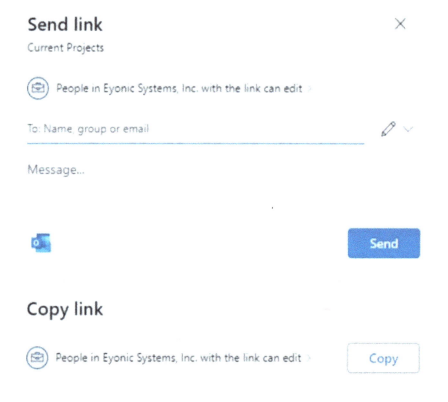

Send link   ×

Current Projects

People in Eyonic Systems, Inc. with the link can edit ›

To: Name, group or email

Message...

Send

Copy link

People in Eyonic Systems, Inc. with the link can edit ›   Copy

2. **Sharing with Specific People**:
- o   After selecting the file or folder, click **"Share"**.
- o   Under **"Send Link"**, enter the email addresses of the people you want to share with. You can also add a message to include with the invitation.

- o You can choose whether recipients can **edit** or just **view** the document.
- o Click **"Send"**.

Desktop App (Windows/Mac)

1. **Sharing via File Explorer/Finder**:
   - o Open your **OneDrive folder** in **File Explorer** (Windows) or **Finder** (Mac).
   - o Right-click the file or folder you want to share, then select **"Share"**.

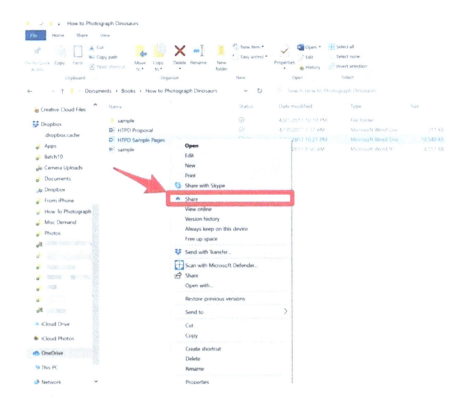

- This opens the **OneDrive Sharing Dialogue** where you can select if you want to send a link or an email invitation to share the file.
- Choose whether the recipients can **edit** or only **view** the file. You can also set a password or expiration date for extra security.

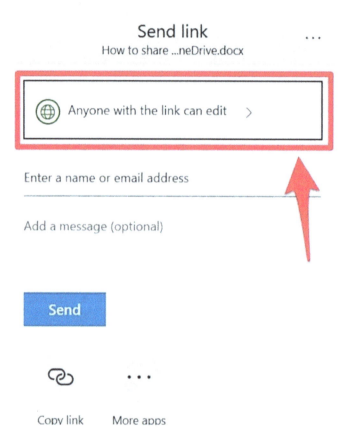

2. **Sharing from the OneDrive App**:
   - Open the **OneDrive** app on your computer.
   - Right-click the file or folder you want to share.

- o Click **"Share"** to open the sharing options, just like the **web interface**.
- o Choose the appropriate sharing settings (edit or view permissions).

Mobile App (iOS & Android)

1. **Sharing Files or Folders**:
   - o Open the **OneDrive app** on your mobile device.
   - o Navigate to the file or folder you want to share.
   - o Tap the **three dots** next to the file/folder and select **"Share"**.
   - o In the sharing window, you can either send a **link** via email or **copy** the link to share elsewhere.
2. **Sharing with Specific People**:
   - o Tap **"Share"** and enter the email addresses of the people you want to share with.
   - o Choose whether they should have **view** or **edit** access.
   - o Tap **"Send"** to share the file/folder.

Setting Permissions: View, Edit, and Collaborate

Once you've shared a file or folder, you can customize permissions to determine who can **view**, **edit**, or **collaborate** on the shared content.

Web Interface (Desktop)

1. **Setting Permissions**:

- After clicking **"Share"**, a link will appear with the default permission set as **"Anyone with the link"**.
- Click on the **"Anyone with the link"** drop-down to adjust permissions.
  - **Can Edit**: If selected, recipients can **edit** the file or folder.
  - **Can View**: If selected, recipients can only **view** the file/folder but cannot make changes.

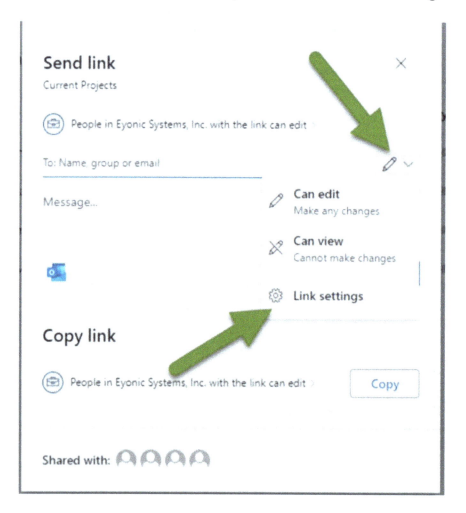

- If you want to further restrict access, you can click on **"More Options"** for additional settings, such as requiring a password or setting an expiration date for the link.

2. **Allowing or Disallowing Editing**:
   - You can disable the **editing** option by selecting **"View Only"** when you are sharing the file or folder. This is perfect if you just want others to access the content without being able to change it.

Desktop App (Windows/Mac)

1. **Modifying Permissions**:
   - Right-click the file or folder in the **OneDrive folder** on **File Explorer** or **Finder**.
   - Select **"Share"**, and you'll be taken to the same **sharing dialogue** you see on the web interface.
   - Change permissions by selecting **"Can Edit"** or **"Can View"**.
   - You can also choose **"Link Settings"** to specify expiration dates or passwords.

Mobile App (iOS & Android)

1. **Setting Permissions**:
   - Tap the **three dots** next to the file/folder in the OneDrive app and select **"Share"**.
   - Tap **"Anyone with the link"** or **"Specific People"** to modify permissions.
   - Select whether recipients can **edit** or **view** the file.

Managing Shared Links

Shared links give others access to your files and folders. Managing these links is essential for keeping track of who has access to your content.

Web Interface (Desktop)

1. **Viewing Shared Links**:
   - On **onedrive.com**, navigate to **"Shared"** in the left-hand menu.
   - Here, you will see all the files and folders you've shared, both with specific people and via links.
2. **Managing or Revoking Links**:
   - Click on the file or folder to open its details.
   - In the **"Manage Access"** section, click on **"Link Settings"** to change the permission level, expiration date, or even **disable** the link entirely.
   - To remove access, click the **"Remove Link"** option.

Desktop App (Windows/Mac)

1. **Managing Links**:
   - Open your **OneDrive folder** on **File Explorer** (Windows) or **Finder** (Mac).
   - Right-click on the shared file and select **"Manage Access"**.
   - You can see all active shared links and permissions here. You can **remove** links or change permissions as needed.

Mobile App (iOS & Android)

1. **Managing Shared Links**:
   - ○ Tap the **three dots** next to the shared file or folder in the OneDrive app.
   - ○ Select **"Manage Access"** to view the links and permissions.
   - ○ If you need to change permissions or remove a link, select the appropriate option from the menu.

Sharing with Specific People vs. Public Links

OneDrive allows you to share files and folders in two primary ways: with **specific people** or through **public links**. Each method has different security and accessibility implications.

Web Interface (Desktop)

1. **Sharing with Specific People**:
   - ○ When sharing with **specific people**, only those you invite via email can access the file or folder.
   - ○ Click **"Share"** and enter the email addresses of those you want to give access.
   - ○ You can restrict this further by requiring users to sign in with a Microsoft account to access the content.
2. **Public Links**:
   - ○ When sharing via **public links**, anyone who has the link can access the file/folder, regardless of whether they have a Microsoft account.
   - ○ For added security, you can set an expiration date or a password for public links.

- This is useful for sharing content widely, such as public documents or presentations, but not ideal for confidential material.

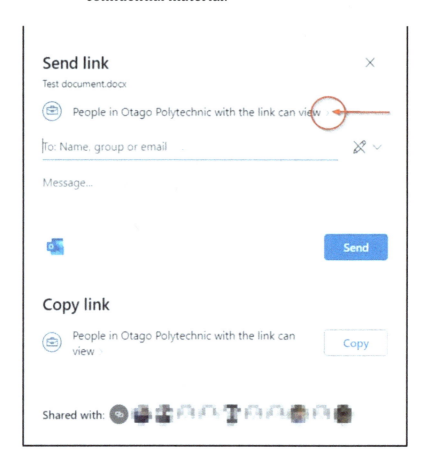

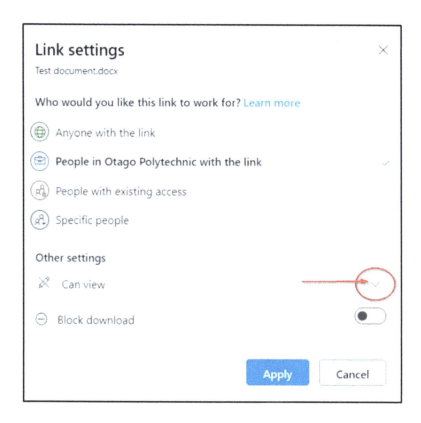

Desktop App (Windows/Mac)

1. **Specific People**:
   - o In the desktop app, right-click the file and choose **"Share"**.
   - o Under **"Link Settings"**, choose **"Specific People"** to send an invitation to select individuals only.
2. **Public Links**:
   - o Similarly, you can select **"Anyone with the link"** to allow anyone who receives the link to access the shared file/folder.

Mobile App (iOS & Android)

1. **Specific People**:
   - Tap **"Share"** and enter the email addresses of specific people to limit access.
   - Recipients must sign in to view or edit the file.
2. **Public Links**:
   - Tap **"Share"** and choose **"Anyone with the link"** to make the link accessible to anyone.

Chapter 6: Syncing Files with OneDrive

Syncing files with OneDrive ensures that your documents, photos, and other files are available across multiple devices, whether online or offline. OneDrive provides an efficient way to keep all your data updated and accessible no matter where you are. In this chapter, we'll cover how to set up OneDrive sync, manage synced files, and troubleshoot common syncing issues.

Setting Up OneDrive Sync

Syncing your files to OneDrive ensures that your files are available across all devices and stored in the cloud, while keeping your local copy updated. This step is particularly useful for easy access and backup.

Web Interface (Desktop)

- **Note**: The web interface does not handle syncing directly. Syncing is primarily done through the desktop app.

Desktop App (Windows)

1. **Installing the OneDrive App**:
   - Ensure you've installed the **OneDrive desktop app**. If not, download and install it from the **Microsoft website**.

- o During installation, the app automatically sets up your sync for the default **OneDrive folder** on your PC.
2. **Linking Your Account**:
   - o After installation, open the **OneDrive** app (you can search for it via the Start menu).
   - o Sign in using your **Microsoft account** (the same account used for OneDrive).
   - o Once logged in, OneDrive will automatically sync your cloud files to your **local OneDrive folder** in **File Explorer** (this is where all your synced files will appear).
3. **Choosing Folders to Sync**:
   - o Once logged in, you'll be asked to select which folders to sync from OneDrive to your PC. Choose the folders that you need or select **"Sync all files and folders in OneDrive"** for a complete sync.
4. **Start Syncing**:
   - o Once you've set your preferences, click **"Start Syncing"** to begin the sync process.
   - o Your files will begin syncing, and you can track progress via the **OneDrive icon** in the taskbar notification area.

Mobile App (iOS & Android)

The mobile app **does not sync files to your phone's local storage** in the same way that the desktop app does. However, you can **access files offline** using the mobile app.

1. **Accessing Files Offline**:

- o Open the **OneDrive mobile app**.
- o Find the file or folder you want to access offline.
- o Tap the **three dots** next to the file/folder and select **"Make Available Offline"**.
- o This will download the file to your mobile device for offline use.

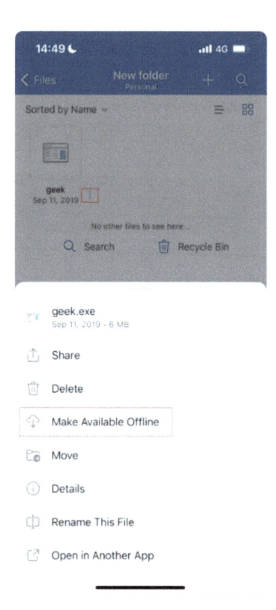

Syncing Files for Offline Access

You can sync files to access them without an internet connection, which is particularly useful for laptops or mobile devices.

Web Interface (Desktop)

- **Web Interface does not support offline syncing**. You must use the **desktop app** for syncing offline files.

Desktop App (Windows)

1. **Using Files On-Demand**:
   - **Files On-Demand** is a OneDrive feature that allows you to see all your files in **File Explorer** without having to download them to your device.
   - By default, OneDrive will sync files and make them available offline only when you open them. These files will be marked with a **cloud icon** (online only) or a **green checkmark** (available offline).
2. **Making Files Always Available Offline**:
   - Right-click the file or folder in **File Explorer** under the **OneDrive** section.
   - Select **"Always Keep on This Device"**.
   - This will download the file to your PC, ensuring it's available offline.
   - These files will have a **solid green checkmark**.
3. **Making Files Online-Only**:
   - Right-click the file or folder and select **"Free Up Space"**.
   - This removes the file from your local drive, but it will still be available via OneDrive online.
   - The file will now show a **cloud icon** in File Explorer, indicating it's **online-only**.

Mobile App (iOS & Android)

1. **Making Files Available Offline**:
    o   Open the **OneDrive mobile app**.
    o   Navigate to the file or folder you want to access offline.
    o   Tap the **three dots** beside the file and select **"Make Available Offline"**.
    o   You can now access the file even when you're not connected to the internet.
2. **Viewing Offline Files**:
    o   To access offline files, simply open the **OneDrive app** and navigate to the **"Offline"** section. Here you'll find all the files you've saved for offline use.

Managing Synced Files on Your Desktop

Managing your synced files involves organizing them, checking sync status, and ensuring everything is up-to-date.

Web Interface (Desktop)

The web interface does not provide direct file management for synced files. For managing synced files, use the **OneDrive desktop app** or **mobile app**.

Desktop App (Windows)

1. **View Sync Status**:
    o   In **File Explorer**, under the **OneDrive** folder, you can view the sync status of your files.

- o Files with a **green checkmark** are synced and available offline.
- o Files with a **blue cloud icon** are only available online and do not take up local storage space.
- o **Red X** indicates there is a syncing error.

2. **Pausing or Resuming Sync**:
   - o Right-click the **OneDrive** icon in the taskbar notification area.
   - o Click **"Pause syncing"** and select the duration for the pause. You can resume syncing at any time by clicking **"Resume syncing"**.

3. **Unlinking OneDrive**:
   - o If you need to stop syncing files temporarily or permanently, right-click the **OneDrive** icon and choose **"Settings"**.
   - o In the **Account** tab, select **"Unlink this PC"**. This will stop syncing your files, but they will remain accessible on OneDrive online.

Mobile App (iOS & Android)

1. **Managing Offline Files**:
   - o Open the **OneDrive mobile app** and navigate to your files.
   - o Tap the **three dots** next to any file and choose **"Remove from Offline"** to free up space on your device.

2. **Viewing Synced Files**:
   - o To see all your synced files, simply go to the **"Offline"** tab in the OneDrive app.

Troubleshooting Syncing Issues

Occasionally, you might encounter issues while syncing files. Below are common problems and how to fix them.

Web Interface (Desktop)

- **No Syncing Functionality**: The web interface does not support direct file syncing. Ensure you're using the **desktop app** for this functionality.

Desktop App (Windows)

1. **Sync Issues Due to Storage Limits**:
   - Ensure you have enough local storage available. If not, clear up space or use **Files On-Demand** to keep files online-only.
2. **Out of Sync or Stuck Files**:
   - Open **OneDrive** by clicking on the **cloud icon** in the taskbar.
   - Check for any syncing errors marked with a **red X**. Right-click the file or folder and select **"View sync problems"** for further instructions.
   - If the file is still not syncing, right-click the **OneDrive** icon and select **"Pause syncing"** for a few minutes, then resume syncing.
3. **Re-signing In to OneDrive**:
   - If syncing issues persist, try **signing out** of the OneDrive app and then signing back in. This can often fix connectivity and sync issues.
4. **Resetting OneDrive**:

o If none of the above fixes work, you can reset OneDrive by pressing **Windows + R** and typing **"%localappdata%\Microsoft\OneDrive\onedriv e.exe /reset"**.

o This will clear any sync issues, but be aware that it may take some time to resync all your files after a reset.

Mobile App (iOS & Android)

1. **Files Not Syncing on Mobile**:

o Ensure you have an **active internet connection** (either Wi-Fi or mobile data).

o Try closing and reopening the OneDrive app.

o If syncing still doesn't work, uninstall and reinstall the app to reset the sync process.

2. **Storage Issues**:

o If your phone is low on space, OneDrive may not sync properly. Consider freeing up space on your device or adjusting your offline file settings.

Chapter 7: Version History and File Recovery

O nedrive provides tools to manage file versions and recover files that might have been lost or corrupted. This chapter will guide you through everything you need to know about **version history** and **file recovery**, ensuring that you can always retrieve the files you need.

Understanding OneDrive's Version History

Version History allows you to view and restore previous versions of a file, ensuring you never lose valuable information due to accidental changes or edits. This feature is essential for maintaining the integrity of your files over time.

Web Interface (Desktop)

1. **Accessing Version History**:
   o Navigate to **OneDrive** on your browser and locate the file you want to manage.
   o Right-click on the file and select **"Version History"**. Alternatively, click the three dots (**More options**) next to the file and select **"Version History"** from the dropdown.

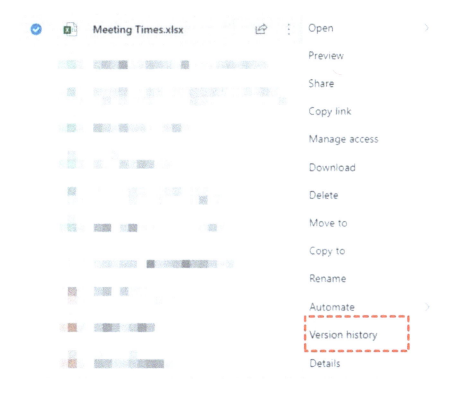

- o A new window will open showing a list of all versions of the file with the **date and time** of the last changes.

2. **Viewing Changes**:
   - o From this menu, you can view the **changes** that have been made to each version. If the version is a document, you will be able to view and compare the text and content of previous versions.

Desktop App (Windows)

1. **Accessing Version History via File Explorer**:
   - o Open **File Explorer** and navigate to your **OneDrive folder**.

- o Right-click the file you want to view the version history for.
- o Select **"Version History"** from the context menu. This will open a version history window where you can see the **file's previous versions**.

2. **Previewing Older Versions**:
   - o In the **Version History** window, you will see older versions listed by date and time. You can select any version and click **"Open"** to preview the file.

3. **Restoring Older Versions**:
   - o To restore a previous version of the file, click on the version you want to restore, then select **"Restore"**.
   - o This action will bring the selected version back as the **current version** of the file, while keeping all other previous versions intact.

Mobile App (iOS & Android)

1. **Accessing Version History**:
   - o The mobile app does not support detailed version history management like the desktop and web interfaces. However, you can still **view and restore versions** of **Microsoft Office documents** (Word, Excel, PowerPoint) through the **Office apps** (Word, Excel, etc.) when connected to OneDrive.

2. **Restoring a Version on Mobile**:
   - o Open the **Office app** (e.g., Word or Excel) where your document is stored.
   - o Tap on **File > Info > Version History**.
   - o Choose a version and tap **Restore** to revert to the earlier version.

Restoring Previous Versions of Files

Sometimes, you may need to restore a file to an earlier version to undo changes or recover lost information. OneDrive makes this process straightforward.

Web Interface (Desktop)

1. **Restoring to a Previous Version**:
   - In **OneDrive** (web), right-click the file you want to restore.
   - Select **"Version History"** to open the history panel.
   - Choose the version you wish to restore, and click **"Restore"**. The file will be replaced with the selected version.

2. **Download a Previous Version**:
   - If you want to keep the older version but not replace the current version, select the version from the history list and click **"Download"**.
   - This allows you to save the older version to your computer while keeping the current version intact.

Desktop App (Windows)

1. **Restoring via File Explorer**:
   - Right-click the file you want to revert to a previous version.
   - Select **"Version History"** from the context menu.
   - In the **Version History** window, choose the version to restore.
   - Click **"Restore"** to replace the file with the selected version.

Mobile App (iOS & Android)

- **Mobile apps** don't have a direct way to restore files to previous versions. However, if you're working with **Microsoft Office documents**, you can restore versions via the **Office apps** like **Word** or **Excel** by tapping on **File > Version History**.

File Recovery in OneDrive

The **File Recovery** feature in OneDrive allows you to recover deleted files, folders, or entire libraries from the OneDrive **Recycle Bin**. If your files are not in the Recycle Bin, you can use OneDrive's **File Recovery** feature to restore files lost due to issues like a virus, accidental deletions, or even ransomware attacks.

Web Interface (Desktop)

1. **Accessing the OneDrive Recycle Bin**:
   - In your **OneDrive web interface**, click the **"Recycle Bin"** link on the left sidebar under the **"Files"** section.

- o Here, you will find any **deleted files or folders** that are still recoverable.

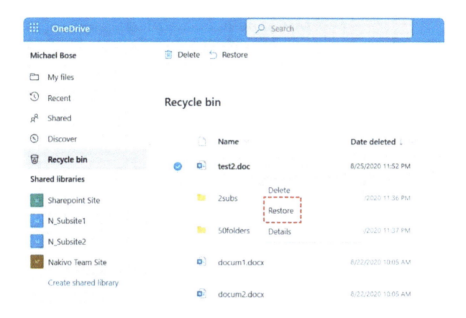

2. **Restoring Deleted Files**:
   - o Browse through the deleted items and select the files or folders you wish to recover.
   - o Click **"Restore"** to restore the selected items to their original location in OneDrive.
   - o If you accidentally delete something, you can always go back to the **Recycle Bin** to recover it.

Desktop App (Windows)

1. **Using File Explorer to Access the Recycle Bin**:
   - o Open **File Explorer** and navigate to your **OneDrive folder**.

- o Right-click and select **"Restore previous versions"** to check for a local version of the file.
- o If the file isn't available in **File Explorer**, go to **OneDrive Online** via the web interface.

2. **File Recovery Using Desktop App**:
   - o Desktop syncing automatically moves deleted files to the **OneDrive Recycle Bin**, which can be restored from the **web interface**.

Mobile App (iOS & Android)

1. **File Recovery on Mobile**:
   - o You cannot access the **Recycle Bin** directly from the mobile app.

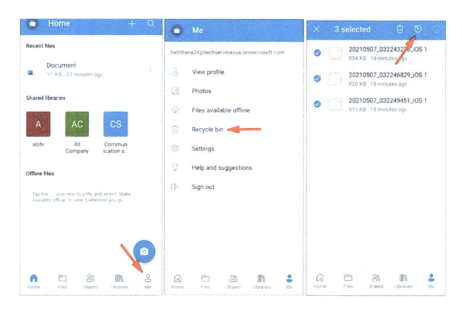

However, you can recover deleted files through the **OneDrive website** or **File Explorer** on your desktop if necessary.

2. **Recovering Files via Office Apps**:
   - ○ If you've deleted an Office document, you can try checking for a backup or version history via the Office apps as mentioned earlier.

Using OneDrive's File Recovery Feature

If your OneDrive account has been compromised (for example, due to a ransomware attack) or you need to restore a large set of deleted files, the **File Recovery Feature** is a powerful tool that can help you recover everything at once.

Web Interface (Desktop)

1. **Using OneDrive's File Recovery Tool**:
   - ○ Open the **OneDrive website** in your browser and go to the **"Settings"** (click on the gear icon in the top-right).
   - ○ Under **"Options"**, select **"Restore your OneDrive"**.
   - ○ You can select a specific **time period** during which you want to restore your files (e.g., the last 30 days, or a custom date range).
   - ○ Follow the instructions to restore all files in your OneDrive to the way they were at that time. This includes any files deleted or modified during the period.

Desktop App (Windows)

- The **File Recovery tool** is primarily accessible through the **web interface**. However, if you have already synced your files, you can restore them using **version history** or by using the **Recycle Bin** in **File Explorer**.

Mobile App (iOS & Android)

- The **File Recovery Tool** is **not available** directly from the **mobile app**. To recover files after an issue, use the **web interface** on a computer or access through **File Explorer** if synced.

Chapter 8: Collaboration in OneDrive

Collaboration is a key feature of **OneDrive**, allowing multiple people to work together on documents in real-time, regardless of their location. Whether you're working on a Word document, Excel spreadsheet, or PowerPoint presentation, **OneDrive** makes it easy to **share, edit, and communicate** with others. In this chapter, we will walk through the steps of **co-authoring, adding comments, tracking changes**, and **notifying collaborators** of updates.

Collaborating on Documents in Real-Time

OneDrive makes it possible for multiple users to edit the same document simultaneously, which is known as **real-time collaboration**. This is an invaluable feature when working with teams or partners on shared documents.

Web Interface (Desktop)

1. **Opening and Sharing a Document for Collaboration:**
   - In your **OneDrive** (web), locate the document you want to collaborate on.
   - Right-click the document and select **"Share"**.
   - Choose the appropriate sharing option (e.g., **"Anyone with the link"**, or **"Specific people"**).
   - After sharing, the document can be edited by the invited users in real time.

2. **Real-Time Collaboration**:
   - Once the document is open in your browser, you will see the names of other collaborators at the top of the screen.
   - Each collaborator will be able to edit the document in real-time. You'll see the changes being made live, and any new edits will appear instantly.
   - You can work together without worrying about conflicting changes, as **OneDrive** saves automatically.

Desktop App (Windows)

1. **Collaborating on Documents Using Microsoft Office Apps**:
   - Open the **OneDrive folder** on your computer and find the document you wish to collaborate on.
   - Double-click the file to open it in the appropriate **Office app** (Word, Excel, or PowerPoint).
   - If the document is stored in OneDrive and others are working on it, you will see their **avatars** at the top of the screen, indicating they are currently editing.
2. **Real-Time Edits**:
   - As changes are made by collaborators, they will appear in real-time on your screen. You'll see their edits highlighted as they type.
   - For **Word** and **Excel**, you'll also see a notification when a collaborator leaves a comment or makes significant changes.

Mobile App (iOS & Android)

1. **Collaborating on Documents Using Office Mobile Apps**:
   - Open the **OneDrive app** and navigate to the document you want to collaborate on.
   - Tap on the file to open it in the relevant **Office mobile app** (Word, Excel, or PowerPoint).
   - If other users are also working on the document, you'll see their **avatars** on the screen.
2. **Real-Time Collaboration**:
   - You can edit the document at the same time as other users, and changes will sync automatically.
   - The app will update with collaborators' changes, though you might not see them in real-time, depending on your internet connection.

Using Microsoft Office Apps for Co-Authoring

Co-authoring allows multiple users to work on the same document at once. It's one of the most powerful features for collaboration, especially when using **Word**, **Excel**, and **PowerPoint**.

Web Interface (Desktop)

1. **Co-Authoring in Word, Excel, and PowerPoint**:
   - Open the document in the **web interface** of **Word**, **Excel**, or **PowerPoint** through OneDrive.
   - Share the document by clicking **Share** and inviting others to co-author. They can open the document in their own browser, and all changes will be visible to everyone editing the document at once.

2. **Viewing Who is Editing**:
   - In the top-right corner of the document, you'll see the names or initials of users who are currently editing the document. If there are multiple users, their changes will be highlighted in different colors.
   - You'll also be able to see who is typing or working in a specific section of the document.

Desktop App (Windows)

1. **Co-Authoring in Desktop Microsoft Office Apps**:
   - Open the document stored in **OneDrive** with **Word**, **Excel**, or **PowerPoint** on your desktop.
   - If other users are collaborating, you'll see their names appear at the top of the document.
   - As users type, you will notice that the document reflects their updates in real-time.

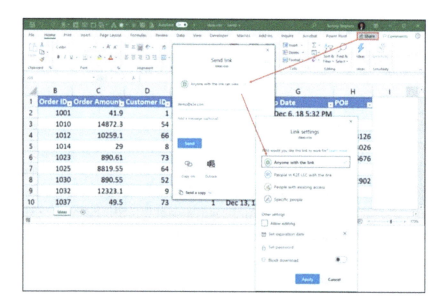

2. **Conflict Resolution**:
   - o If two collaborators try to edit the same section at once, **OneDrive** will attempt to merge the changes automatically. If there's a conflict, the document will prompt you to review and resolve it manually.

Mobile App (iOS & Android)

1. **Co-Authoring on Mobile Devices**:
   - o Open the document in the **Office mobile app**.
   - o As long as others are editing, you will see their initials or profile pictures at the top of the screen.
   - o If you are connected to the internet, all changes will sync in real-time as you collaborate.
2. **Editing on Mobile**:
   - o You can make edits as usual, but real-time collaboration is not as fluid on mobile devices as it is on desktops or the web. Changes will update when syncing, and you'll see collaborator changes when the app refreshes.

Adding Comments and Track Changes

OneDrive and Office apps support **comments** and **track changes**, which are essential tools for reviewing and providing feedback.

Web Interface (Desktop)

1. **Adding Comments**:
   - o Open your document in the **OneDrive** web app (via **Word**, **Excel**, or **PowerPoint**).

- Highlight the text or section you want to comment on.
- Right-click and select **"New Comment"** or click the comment icon on the toolbar.

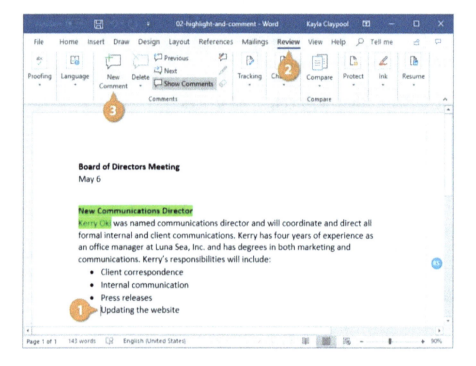

- Type your comment, and collaborators will be able to see it in the right-hand sidebar.

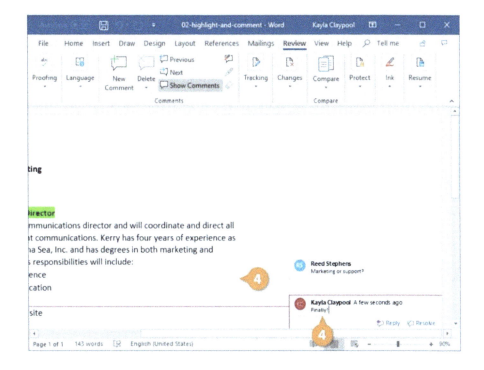

2. **Tracking Changes**:
   - ○ In **Word** and **Excel**, click on **Review > Track Changes** to enable this feature.
   - ○ All edits made by collaborators will be visible in the document, marked by underlines, strikethroughs, or color coding.

Desktop App (Windows)

1. **Adding Comments in Microsoft Office Apps**:
   - ○ Open your document in **Word**, **Excel**, or **PowerPoint**.
   - ○ Highlight the text or content to comment on and go to the **Review** tab in the ribbon.

- ○ Click **New Comment** to add your input.
- ○ Collaborators can reply to comments, creating an ongoing conversation.
2. **Tracking Changes**:
   - ○ Enable **Track Changes** under the **Review** tab. Every change made to the document will be tracked, making it easier to see what was modified and by whom.

Mobile App (iOS & Android)

1. **Adding Comments on Mobile**:
   - ○ Open your document in the **Office mobile app**.
   - ○ Tap and hold the text you want to comment on.
   - ○ Select **Insert Comment**, type your message, and tap **Done**.
2. **Track Changes on Mobile**:
   - ○ Currently, **Track Changes** is not fully supported in the mobile apps. However, comments can still be added in documents, and changes will appear as synced updates when you view the document later on other platforms.

Notifying Collaborators of Changes

To ensure smooth collaboration, **OneDrive** allows you to notify collaborators whenever changes are made to shared files or documents.

Web Interface (Desktop)

1. **Notifying Collaborators via Email**:
   - When sharing a document, select the **"Send Email"** checkbox to notify collaborators.
   - You can customize the message to let collaborators know about recent changes or updates.
2. **Managing Notifications**:
   - Go to **Settings** > **Notifications** to manage how and when you want to be notified about changes made to your shared files.

Desktop App (Windows)

1. **Email Notifications**:
   - If the document is shared, you'll receive email notifications for any changes or comments made by collaborators.
   - You can manage notifications in **OneDrive Settings** under **"Notifications"**.

Mobile App (iOS & Android)

1. **Push Notifications**:
   - On mobile, **OneDrive** will send push notifications for document edits or comments, depending on your notification settings.
2. **Email Notifications**:
   - If you've shared the file and want collaborators to be notified, ensure email notifications are enabled from the **OneDrive web interface**.

Chapter 9: Advanced OneDrive Features

Onedrive offers a variety of advanced features that allow you to optimize file management, collaborate efficiently, and secure your data. In this chapter, we will walk through several **advanced features** that will enhance your experience, particularly in a professional or business context.

Setting Up Auto-Save and Backup

Auto-Save and Backup are crucial for ensuring that your work is always backed up, minimizing the risk of data loss.

Web Interface (Desktop)

1. **Setting Up Auto-Save**:
   - Open a document in **OneDrive** through **Word, Excel,** or **PowerPoint** on the web.
   - By default, **Auto-Save** is enabled for documents stored in **OneDrive**. This ensures that any changes you make are automatically saved to the cloud as you work.
   - There's no need to click **Save**—all updates are saved instantly in the cloud.
   - To ensure Auto-Save is on, check for a **"Saved"** message next to the document title at the top of the screen.
2. **Backup Settings**:

- o OneDrive for personal use automatically backs up your **Desktop**, **Documents**, and **Pictures** folders. You can customize which folders are included by going to **Settings** > **Backup** > **Manage Backup**.
- o Ensure these folders are selected for backup, and your files will be stored in the cloud automatically.

Desktop App (Windows)

1. **Setting Up Auto-Save**:
   - o Open **OneDrive** on your desktop and go to **OneDrive Settings** by right-clicking the OneDrive icon in the taskbar.
   - o Under the **Backup** tab, ensure **Auto-Save** is enabled for **Documents** and **Pictures** folders. You can also include other folders for backup as needed.
   - o Click **Start Backup** to begin syncing these folders to OneDrive automatically.
2. **Backup Your Files**:
   - o Ensure **OneDrive** is syncing your selected folders by looking for the cloud icon next to your files. Files that are backed up will have a cloud icon, while files that are locally available will show a green checkmark.

Mobile App (iOS & Android)

1. **Setting Up Auto-Save for Photos and Videos**:
   - o Open the **OneDrive app** on your mobile device.
   - o Go to **Settings** > **Camera Upload** and enable the **Auto-upload** feature. This will automatically upload

your photos and videos to OneDrive when you connect to Wi-Fi.

- o Choose whether to upload **all photos** or only those you take with the app.
2. **Backup Photos and Videos**:
   - o The **Camera Upload** feature will continuously back up your photos and videos to OneDrive, so you never have to worry about manually uploading them again.

Managing Storage Space in OneDrive

As you use OneDrive, it's essential to keep track of your storage space to ensure you don't run out of room, especially if you store many files or large documents.

Web Interface (Desktop)

1. **Checking Storage Space**:
   - o Go to the **OneDrive** web interface and click on your **profile icon** in the top-right corner.
   - o Select **"Settings"** and then **"Options"**. Under the **"Storage"** section, you'll see how much space you've used and how much is available.
   - o If you're nearing your limit, you can upgrade your plan to get more storage, or delete old files that are no longer needed.
2. **Managing Storage**:
   - o You can click on **"Manage Storage"** to access more detailed options, such as viewing large files, emptying the **Recycle Bin**, and checking for duplicate files that may be taking up unnecessary space.

Desktop App (Windows)

1. **Monitoring Storage**:
   - Right-click the **OneDrive** icon in your taskbar, then select **"Settings"** > **"Account"** to view how much storage you have used and available.
   - If you're running low on space, you can **move files** out of OneDrive or delete files to free up space.
2. **Freeing Up Space**:
   - Use the **"Files On-Demand"** feature to store files online instead of locally. Right-click any file in your OneDrive folder and select **"Free up space"**. The file will remain in the cloud but will not take up space on your hard drive.

Mobile App (iOS & Android)

1. **Checking Storage on Mobile**:
   - Open the **OneDrive app**, then go to **Settings** > **Account** to see how much storage you have used on your mobile device.
2. **Managing Storage**:
   - You can remove files that have already been uploaded to OneDrive, or use the **Files On-Demand** feature to save space by downloading files only when needed.

Integrating OneDrive with Microsoft Teams

Integration with **Microsoft Teams** makes it easier to share, collaborate, and manage your files directly within Teams channels or conversations.

Web Interface (Desktop)

1. **Using OneDrive in Teams**:
   - In **Microsoft Teams**, you can access your **OneDrive** files directly within a chat or channel.
   - When creating a new conversation or chat, click the **Attach** button (paperclip icon), select **OneDrive**, and choose the file you want to share.
2. **Collaborating on Documents**:
   - Once the file is shared, team members can collaborate in real-time directly within the Teams app. All changes are saved back to OneDrive automatically.

Desktop App (Windows)

1. **Integrating OneDrive with Teams**:
   - Open **Microsoft Teams** on your desktop and navigate to the channel or chat where you want to share a file.
   - Click on the **Files** tab and choose **OneDrive** to find and upload the file from your OneDrive.

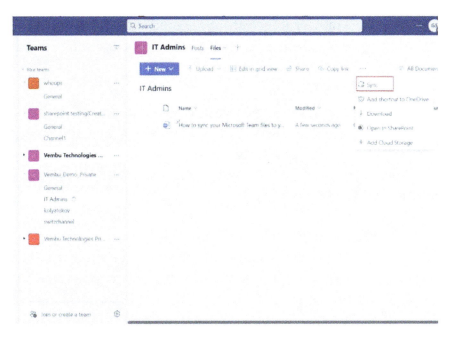

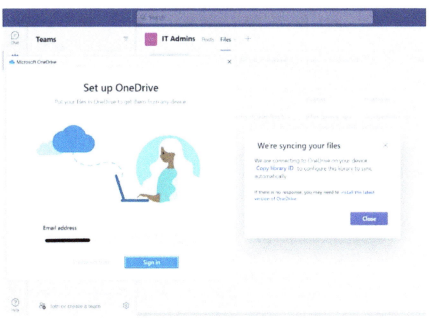

o   Collaborators can open, edit, and comment on the document within Teams, and changes will sync back to OneDrive.

2. **Real-Time Editing**:
   o   Just like in OneDrive, multiple team members can edit a document stored in Teams, and the changes will appear in real time.

Mobile App (iOS & Android)

1. **Using OneDrive Files in Teams Mobile**:
   o   In the **Teams app**, tap on **Files** and select **OneDrive** to access and share files stored in your OneDrive account.
   o   You can also access files shared in **Teams channels** and **chats** from your **OneDrive**.

2. **Collaborating on Documents**:
   o   When working on documents in the mobile version of Teams, all changes are synced with OneDrive in real-time, just like on desktop.

Using OneDrive for Business (Enterprise Features)

OneDrive for Business is an enterprise-level version of OneDrive with additional features tailored to business users.

Web Interface (Desktop)

1. **Understanding OneDrive for Business**:
   o   OneDrive for Business offers advanced file sharing and management features, including **file retention**

policies, **data loss prevention**, and **eDiscovery** capabilities.

- o You can access your **Business OneDrive** from the **Office 365** portal and use it to share files with team members while maintaining security controls.

2. **Using Advanced Features**:
   - o Admins can manage user permissions, assign roles, and control who has access to shared files.
   - o Integration with tools like **SharePoint** and **Microsoft Teams** further enhances collaboration and file management.

Desktop App (Windows)

1. **Managing Business Documents**:
   - o Open **OneDrive for Business** on your desktop and manage your files just like in personal OneDrive, but with the added benefit of enterprise security and permissions.
   - o Collaborate on documents with teammates while ensuring that only authorized users can view and edit certain files.

2. **Syncing Business Files**:
   - o Business files sync just like personal files, but may have additional compliance and retention rules applied by your organization's IT department.

Mobile App (iOS & Android)

1. **Accessing Business Files**:

- o Open the **OneDrive app** and sign in using your **business account** to access your OneDrive for Business files.
- o Share and collaborate on documents with your coworkers, all while adhering to your company's data security policies.

2. **Mobile Security**:
   - o You may need to use additional **multi-factor authentication** (MFA) for logging in to your **OneDrive for Business** account, ensuring the security of corporate data.

Part II: Getting Started with SharePoint

Chapter 10: Introduction to SharePoint

SharePoint is a powerful collaboration and document management platform developed by Microsoft. It provides teams and organizations with a centralized location to store, organize, share, and manage content, knowledge, and applications. In this chapter, we'll break down the essential aspects of SharePoint and its relationship to OneDrive, focusing on key differences, types of SharePoint sites, and how SharePoint supports collaboration.

What is SharePoint?

SharePoint is a web-based platform used by businesses and organizations to manage documents, data, and content across teams and departments. It allows users to create, store, and share content, as well as collaborate in real-time. Key features of SharePoint include:

- **Document Management**: SharePoint helps store documents in a secure, easily accessible way, with built-in version control.
- **Collaboration**: It allows teams to collaborate on documents, manage tasks, and track changes in real time.
- **Customizable Sites**: Users can create custom sites that fit specific needs, whether for managing documents, running workflows, or sharing information.

- **Integration with Microsoft 365**: SharePoint integrates seamlessly with other Microsoft tools like **Teams, Outlook, Word**, and **Excel** to enhance productivity.

SharePoint vs. OneDrive: Key Differences

While both **SharePoint** and **OneDrive** are cloud-based services provided by Microsoft, they are designed for different purposes and have distinct features.

OneDrive:

- **Personal Cloud Storage**: OneDrive is designed for personal file storage. It's ideal for individual use, offering features like file syncing, sharing, and collaboration.
- **Focus on Individual Users**: Each user has their own **OneDrive** account where they store files, and files are shared on a one-to-one or small group basis.
- **Limited Sharing Options**: While files can be shared with others, OneDrive is primarily focused on personal use, and collaboration is more informal.

SharePoint:

- **Collaboration & Document Management**: SharePoint is focused on team and organization-wide collaboration. It allows teams to create **sites** for storing and managing shared documents, data, and projects.
- **Team-Oriented**: SharePoint is best for team and project collaboration, providing tools for managing workflows,

organizing documents, and tracking tasks at a broader organizational level.

- **Enterprise-Level Features**: SharePoint includes advanced features like **workflows**, **document approval processes**, and **enterprise search**, which are tailored for large businesses.

Feature	OneDrive	SharePoint
Primary Use	Personal cloud storage	Team collaboration and document management
User Focus	Individual	Teams, Departments, Organizations
Sharing	Personal sharing with individuals or groups	Team-wide and organization-wide sharing
Storage Type	Personal files	Shared files for team or project use
Customization	Limited	Highly customizable (sites, lists, libraries)
Collaboration	Basic (real-time document editing)	Advanced (document management, workflows, team tasks)

Types of SharePoint Sites: Team Sites vs. Communication Sites

SharePoint allows users to create different types of sites depending on the purpose of the site. Two of the most common site types are **Team Sites** and **Communication Sites**.

Team Sites:

- **Purpose**: Designed for collaboration within a specific team or group. Team sites help organize documents, discussions, tasks, and calendars.
- **Usage**: Ideal for projects, departments, and small teams that need to work together and share resources.
- **Key Features**:

- Document libraries to store and manage shared documents.
- Lists and task management tools for tracking project progress.
- **Integration with Microsoft Teams**: Team sites can be directly connected to Teams, allowing for seamless collaboration between the two.

Communication Sites:

- **Purpose**: Designed to share information across the organization, such as company news, announcements, and important documents.
- **Usage**: Ideal for one-way communication, such as sharing policies, procedures, or corporate updates with a wide audience.
- **Key Features**:
  - Attractive, visual layouts that allow for easy publishing of content.
  - Focused on delivering information in a digestible format.
  - Great for content-heavy sites like company intranets or HR portals.

Site Type	Team Site	Communication Site
Purpose	Collaboration within teams	Sharing information across organizations
Focus	Document management, tasks, discussions	Announcements, corporate content
Audience	Team members and collaborators	Large groups or entire organizations
Customization	Highly customizable for specific teams	Focused on presentation and content display
Best Use	Team projects and document sharing	Company news, events, and public announcements

Understanding SharePoint's Role in Collaboration and Document Management

SharePoint plays a central role in facilitating collaboration within teams and organizations. By offering advanced features for **document management**, **content sharing**, and **team collaboration**, SharePoint provides organizations with the tools needed to work together efficiently and securely. Here's how SharePoint supports collaboration and document management:

Collaboration:

- **Document Co-Authoring**: Multiple team members can work on the same document at the same time, making real-time edits, comments, and suggestions. SharePoint integrates with Microsoft Office apps like **Word**, **Excel**, and **PowerPoint** to enable smooth co-authoring experiences.
- **Shared Calendars & Tasks**: Teams can share calendars, assign tasks, and track deadlines directly within SharePoint, ensuring everyone is on the same page.

- **Real-Time Notifications**: SharePoint sends notifications about document changes, updates, and comments, helping teams stay up-to-date on collaborative efforts.

Document Management:

- **Version Control**: SharePoint automatically tracks versions of documents, allowing teams to revert to previous versions when needed.
- **Document Approval**: SharePoint supports document workflows and approval processes, helping organizations maintain proper content governance.
- **Search and Metadata**: SharePoint has robust search capabilities, making it easy to locate documents and files based on metadata or keywords.

Chapter 11: Setting Up SharePoint

S etting up **SharePoint** properly is crucial to ensure smooth collaboration and document management within your team or organization. In this chapter, we will guide you through creating a SharePoint account, setting up your first SharePoint site, choosing the right site type, and configuring settings based on your needs.

1. Creating a SharePoint Account

Before you can create a SharePoint site, you need a **Microsoft 365 account** because **SharePoint** is part of the Microsoft 365 suite. If you don't have one already, follow these steps to create your account:

For Desktop (Web Interface):

1. Open your web browser and go to https://www.office.com.
2. Click on **Sign Up** or **Sign In** (if you already have a Microsoft 365 account).
3. Follow the on-screen instructions to create your Microsoft account using your email and password.
4. Once your account is created, you'll have access to **SharePoint** and other Microsoft 365 apps like OneDrive, Teams, Word, and Excel.

For Mobile Devices (iOS/Android):

1. Download and install the **Microsoft Office** app from the App Store (iOS) or Google Play Store (Android).
2. Open the app and sign in with your Microsoft 365 account or create one using the **Sign Up** option.
3. After signing in, tap the **SharePoint** icon to start using it on your mobile device.

2. Creating Your First SharePoint Site

Once your Microsoft 365 account is set up, you can create a **SharePoint site** for collaboration or content management. Follow the steps below:

For Desktop (Web Interface):

1. Log in to your **Microsoft 365 account** and go to the **SharePoint** app.

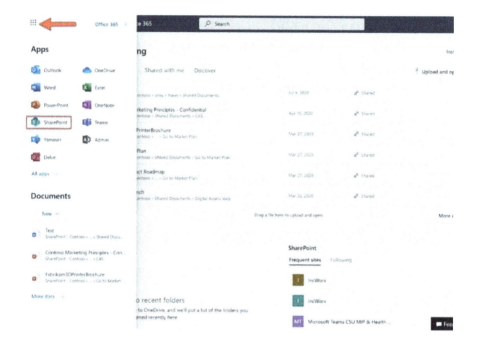

2. On the **SharePoint homepage**, click on **Create Site** at the top.

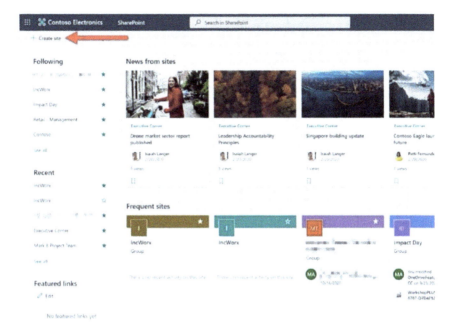

3. You will be prompted to choose between two types of sites:
    o **Team Site**: Choose this if you want to collaborate on documents and projects with your team.
    o **Communication Site**: Choose this for sharing content with a wider audience, such as company-wide announcements.

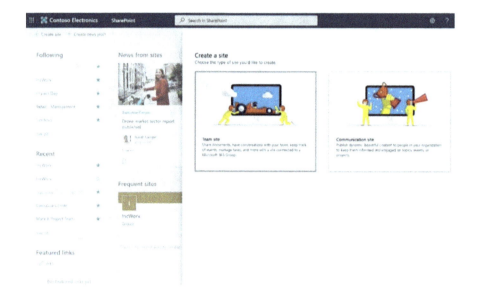

4. Enter a **Site Name**, **Description**, and **Privacy Settings** (whether the site will be public or private).

5. Click **Next**, and SharePoint will create your site.

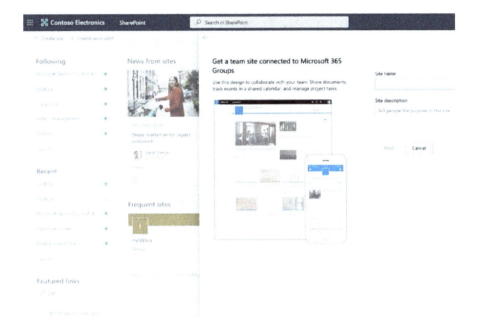

6. You will be directed to your newly created **SharePoint site** where you can start adding content.

For Mobile Devices (iOS/Android):

1. Open the **Microsoft Office** app.
2. Tap on the **SharePoint** icon.
3. Tap the **+ (plus)** button or the **Create Site** option.
4. Choose whether to create a **Team Site** or **Communication Site** based on your needs.
5. Follow the prompts to set the **Site Name** and **Description**.
6. Tap **Create** to finish.

3. Choosing Between Team Sites and Communication Sites

When creating a SharePoint site, you'll need to decide between a **Team Site** and a **Communication Site**. Here's a breakdown of when to use each:

Team Sites:

- **Purpose**: Team Sites are ideal for small groups or project teams that need to collaborate on documents and tasks.
- **Best For**: Collaboration on documents, tracking projects, sharing files and resources within a team.
- **Key Features**:
  - Document libraries for storing shared files.
  - Lists to manage tasks, deadlines, and projects.
  - Integrated with **Microsoft Teams** for chat and video conferencing.

Communication Sites:

- **Purpose**: Communication Sites are designed for broadcasting information to a large audience, like company-wide updates or announcements.
- **Best For**: Public-facing content, such as news, events, or organizational announcements.
- **Key Features**:
  - Beautiful, visually rich pages.
  - Less emphasis on collaboration and more on content presentation.
  - Ideal for intranets, blogs, or corporate news sites.

Choosing the Right Site:

- **For small teams working on projects**: Choose a **Team Site**.
- **For broadcasting information to a wide audience**: Choose a **Communication Site**.

4. Configuring Your Site's Settings

Once your SharePoint site is created, you'll want to configure its settings to meet your specific needs. The settings available may differ based on whether you're using a **Team Site** or a **Communication Site**.

For Desktop (Web Interface):

1. Navigate to your **SharePoint site**.
2. On the top-right corner, click the **Settings (gear icon)**.
3. Select **Site Settings**. This will take you to the settings page, where you can configure the following:
   - **General Settings**: Change the **site name**, **description**, **privacy settings**, and **site theme**.
   - **Permissions**: Set permissions for who can access and modify content on the site. You can add users or groups and assign them roles like **Owner**, **Member**, or **Visitor**.
   - **Navigation**: Configure the navigation menus for easier access to key areas of your site, such as document libraries or lists.

- ○ **Site Features**: Turn on or off various features, such as **Version History, External Sharing**, and **Content Approval**.
4. After adjusting your settings, click **Save** to apply the changes.

For Mobile Devices (iOS/Android):

1. Open the **Microsoft Office** app and tap the **SharePoint** icon.
2. Tap on the **Site** you want to configure.
3. Tap the **Settings** icon (gear icon) in the top-right corner.
4. From here, you can manage basic settings like **site name** and **permissions**, but many advanced settings are best configured through the desktop interface.

Chapter 12: Navigating SharePoint

Efficiently navigating **SharePoint** is essential for finding and managing documents, collaborating with team members, and customizing your site to suit your needs. In this chapter, we will take a detailed look at the **SharePoint interface**, how to understand and work with **Document Libraries** and **Lists**, and how to customize your SharePoint view to make navigation easier.

1. Exploring the SharePoint Interface

The **SharePoint interface** can seem overwhelming at first, but with the right guidance, you'll soon be able to find and organize everything with ease. SharePoint has a consistent layout across devices, but there are some differences in how it appears on desktop, web, and mobile.

For Desktop (Web Interface):

1. Log in to **Microsoft 365** and select **SharePoint** from the app launcher.
2. The main page shows **SharePoint sites** you're a part of, with an option to **Browse all sites**.
3. Once you enter a specific site, the interface consists of the following elements:
    - **Navigation Bar**: This is typically on the left side, where you can access the site's **home page**,

document libraries, lists, and any **other apps** added to the site.

- o **Top Menu**: This menu gives access to actions like **Create**, **Site Settings**, **Share**, etc.
- o **Content Area**: This is where the main content of the site is displayed. Depending on the site, you might see lists of documents, news, announcements, and more.

4. Explore different sections by clicking on the links or tiles, and get used to the flow of navigation.

For Mobile Devices (iOS/Android):

1. Open the **Microsoft Office** app and tap the **SharePoint** icon.
2. You will be shown a list of the **SharePoint sites** you have access to.
3. Tap on a site to view its contents. The **SharePoint mobile interface** is simplified compared to the desktop but still contains the following elements:
   - o **Navigation Menu**: Tap the **hamburger menu (three lines)** in the top-left to access the navigation options, such as documents and lists.
   - o **Content Area**: The main area where you can see news, documents, lists, and any updates on the site.
4. Tap on items or documents to view and interact with them directly on your mobile device.

2. Understanding Document Libraries and Lists

Document Libraries and **Lists** are key components in SharePoint, allowing you to store documents and organize data in a structured way. Let's explore both in detail.

Document Libraries:

A **Document Library** is where files are stored and managed. You can upload, organize, and share documents within a library.

For Desktop (Web Interface):

1. From your SharePoint site, navigate to the **Documents** section in the left-hand **Navigation Bar**.
2. Here, you'll see the default document library called **Documents**, but you can also create new libraries by clicking on **New > Document Library**.

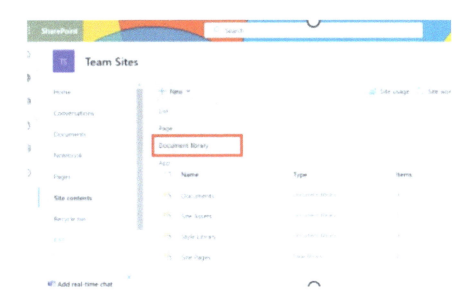

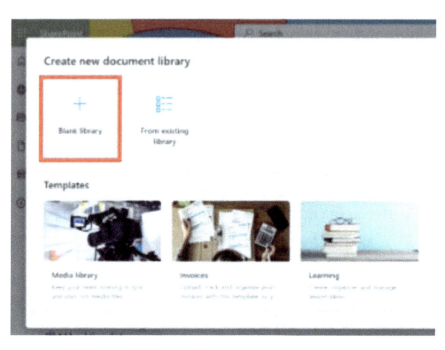

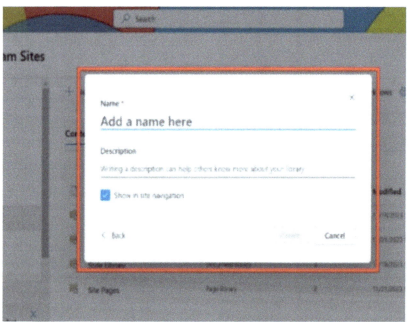

3. Inside the document library, you can:
   - o **Upload Files**: Click **Upload** to add files or folders from your computer.
   - o **Organize Files**: Create **folders** to organize your documents.
   - o **Check In/Out**: If you're using version control, you can check in or check out files to prevent simultaneous edits.

For Mobile Devices (iOS/Android):

1. From the **SharePoint** app, tap on a site to access its documents.
2. Tap on **Documents** to access the document library.
3. To upload a document, tap the **+ (plus)** button, then select **Upload** and choose the file from your device.

Lists:

A **List** in SharePoint is similar to a database, where you can store and manage data in rows and columns. Lists are typically used to manage tasks, issues, or inventory.

For Desktop (Web Interface):

1. To access a list, go to your SharePoint site and select **Site Contents** from the left-hand menu.
2. You'll see a section for **Lists**, where you can view existing lists or create new ones.
3. To create a new list, click **New > List**, then either create a custom list or choose from templates like **Task List**, **Issue Tracking**, or **Event List**.

115

4. You can add new entries by clicking **New Item**, and then entering the data in the list columns.

For Mobile Devices (iOS/Android):

1. Tap on **Lists** from your **SharePoint site** to see available lists.
2. Tap on a list to view its items. You can also add a new item by tapping the **+ (plus)** button, entering the data, and saving it.

3. Accessing Sites and Libraries

As you use SharePoint, you may need to switch between different sites or libraries. Here's how to access them:

For Desktop (Web Interface):

1. From the **SharePoint home page**, you can quickly switch between different sites you have access to by clicking the **Sites** button in the top-left corner.
2. To access a specific **Document Library** within a site, click the site name in the **Sites** list and then navigate to the **Documents** section.

For Mobile Devices (iOS/Android):

1. Open the **SharePoint app** and tap the **Sites** button at the bottom to switch between different sites.
2. Tap on a site to view its libraries or lists. Tap on **Documents** to open the document library associated with that site.

4. Customizing Your SharePoint View

Customization allows you to organize and tailor the way you view content in SharePoint. You can filter, sort, and adjust the display settings to make navigation easier.

For Desktop (Web Interface):

1. **Custom Views for Document Libraries**:
   - In a document library, click the **View Options** (usually on the top-right) and select **Create View**.
   - You can choose a **Standard View**, **Datasheet View**, or **Calendar View** depending on your needs.
   - Add filters and sort options to display files in the order and format that works best for you.
2. **Customizing the Navigation**:
   - Go to **Site Settings** > **Navigation** to reorder or add links to the site's navigation.
   - Add links to frequently accessed libraries, lists, or external sites.
3. **Personalized Dashboards**:
   - You can use **Web Parts** to display content on the homepage, such as documents, calendars, or task lists.

For Mobile Devices (iOS/Android):

1. **Customizing Views**: While customization is more limited on mobile, you can still:
   - Use the search bar at the top to quickly find files or documents.

o Pin frequently accessed sites or libraries to the **home screen** for easy access.
2. **Navigation**: Tap on the **hamburger menu** (three lines) to access your personalized SharePoint content like favorite sites or pinned documents.

Chapter 13: Working with Document Libraries

D ocument Libraries in SharePoint are essential for organizing and storing your files. SharePoint libraries provide powerful features to manage documents and allow for real-time collaboration with others. This chapter will provide a step-by-step guide on how to work effectively with **Document Libraries**.

1. Uploading Documents to SharePoint Libraries

Uploading documents to SharePoint libraries is easy and allows you to store and share files with others. There are a few different methods depending on the device you are using.

For Desktop (Web Interface):

1. Navigate to your **SharePoint site** and click on **Documents** in the left-hand navigation menu to access your document library.
2. In the document library, click **Upload** in the top menu, and then select **Files** or **Folder** depending on what you want to upload.
3. **Select files or folders** from your computer to upload them to SharePoint.

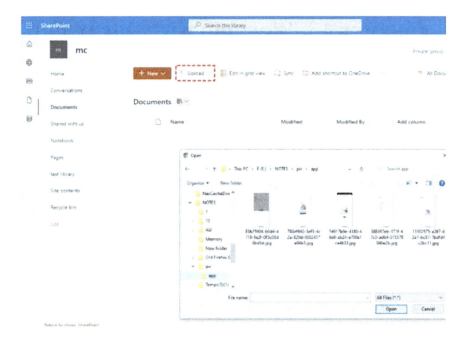

4. Alternatively, you can **drag and drop** files or folders directly into the document library.

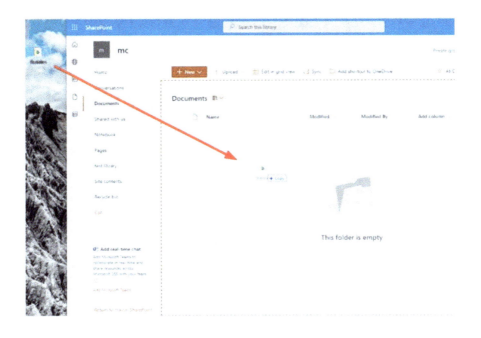

5. Once the files are uploaded, you'll see them listed in the document library. You can now organize them or set up permissions.

For Mobile Devices (iOS/Android):

1. Open the **SharePoint app** and navigate to the document library where you want to upload files.
2. Tap the **+ (plus)** icon at the bottom of the screen, then choose **Upload**.
3. Select files from your device or cloud storage, such as **OneDrive**, to upload them to the SharePoint library.
4. Once uploaded, the files will appear in the document library, and you can start managing them.

2. Organizing Files in Libraries with Folders and Metadata

SharePoint libraries allow for organizing files efficiently using **folders** and **metadata**. Folders are used for a traditional hierarchical organization, while metadata helps categorize documents with tags or labels.

Using Folders:

1. To create a folder, navigate to the document library and click **New > Folder**.
2. Give your folder a name and click **Create**. Now you can drag and drop documents into folders or upload them directly into folders.
3. You can organize folders hierarchically by creating subfolders within folders to create a folder structure for your documents.

Using Metadata:

1. Metadata refers to additional information or tags that describe documents. You can use metadata to classify files, making them easier to find later.
2. To use metadata, first make sure your library has a **Content Type** with predefined columns (metadata fields). For example, a document library for contracts may have columns like **Contract Type**, **Date Signed**, and **Client Name**.
3. When uploading or editing a document, fill in the metadata fields according to the information you want to capture. This

helps with organizing and searching documents more efficiently.

4. In SharePoint, you can also add **managed metadata**, which provides a controlled vocabulary for tags (like selecting predefined tags for classification).

3. Checking In/Out Documents in SharePoint

The **Check In/Check Out** feature in SharePoint is useful when working collaboratively on documents. This feature allows users to lock a document while they are editing it, preventing other users from making changes at the same time.

For Desktop (Web Interface):

1. In your SharePoint document library, locate the document you want to check out.
2. Right-click on the document (or click the ellipsis "..." next to the document name) and select **Check Out**. This locks the document for your use.

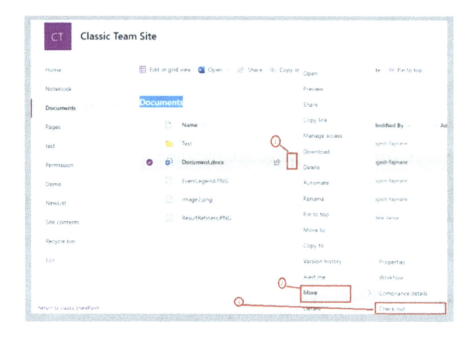

3. Once you've finished editing the document, you can check it back in by right-clicking on the document and selecting **Check In**.

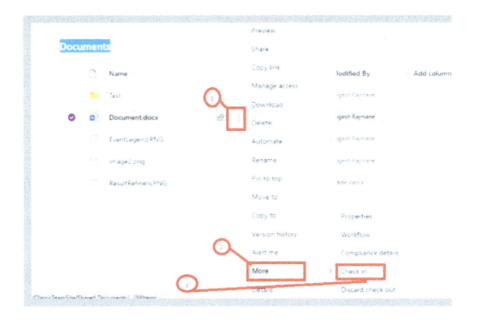

4. If you want to add comments about the changes you made, you can do so when checking the document back in. Click **Check In**, and you'll see an option to **Add a comment**.
5. Once checked in, the document is available for others to edit.

For Mobile Devices (iOS/Android):

1. Open the **SharePoint app** and navigate to your document library.
2. Find the document you want to check out and tap on the document.
3. You should see the **Check Out** option (usually available via the **three-dot menu**). Tap it to check out the document.
4. After editing, tap **Check In** to make the document available for others to edit.

4. Managing File Versions in SharePoint Libraries

Versioning in SharePoint allows you to keep track of changes made to documents over time. You can view previous versions, restore earlier versions, or delete versions when needed.

For Desktop (Web Interface):

1. Navigate to the document library containing the file whose version history you want to view.
2. Right-click on the document (or click the ellipsis "...") and select **Version History**.
3. A window will open displaying all previous versions of the document, including the date and author of each version.
4. To restore a previous version, click on the **Restore** link next to the version you want to revert to.
5. If you wish to delete older versions, select the version(s) and click **Delete**. Be careful when deleting versions, as it's irreversible.

For Mobile Devices (iOS/Android):

1. In the **SharePoint app**, tap on the document whose version history you want to access.
2. Tap the **three-dot menu** (ellipsis), then select **Version History**.
3. From here, you can view previous versions and restore them, similar to the desktop version history feature.
4. Deleting versions might not be possible on mobile devices, so use the web or desktop app for that functionality.

Tips for Managing Document Libraries:

- **Searchability**: Use metadata to make your documents easily searchable. Adding key metadata terms (like client names, dates, or document types) helps others find files quickly.
- **Permissions**: Ensure that only the right people have access to sensitive documents by setting up custom permissions for each document or folder.
- **Version Control**: Enable versioning for all document libraries to ensure changes are tracked and documents can be reverted if necessary.

Chapter 14: Managing SharePoint Permissions

Sharepoint offers a robust and flexible permissions system that allows you to control who can view, edit, and manage your sites and content. Permissions in SharePoint can be set at multiple levels, such as at the site level, document library level, or even for individual files.

1. Understanding Permissions and Security in SharePoint

Permissions in SharePoint are used to define who can access and perform actions on content within your SharePoint site. These permissions are essential for maintaining the security and confidentiality of your organization's data.

Permission Levels:

In SharePoint, permissions are granted through **permission levels**, which are predefined sets of actions a user can perform. Common permission levels include:

- **Full Control**: Can manage everything within a site.
- **Design**: Can create lists and libraries, edit pages, and manage site navigation.
- **Edit**: Can add, edit, and delete content in a site.
- **Contribute**: Can add and edit content but cannot delete it.

- **Read**: Can only view content; no editing privileges.
- **Limited Access**: Can access specific content but not the entire site or library.

SharePoint Security Groups:

Permissions are assigned to users through **SharePoint groups**, which are collections of users. Groups allow administrators to easily assign permissions to multiple users at once, instead of setting permissions individually.

Common SharePoint groups include:

- **Owners**: Full Control permission level.
- **Members**: Edit permission level.
- **Visitors**: Read permission level.

2. Setting Permissions for Users and Groups

SharePoint allows you to assign permissions to individual users or groups. Permissions can be set at the site, library, folder, or file level, and are inherited by default. You can break inheritance if you need custom permissions for specific users or groups.

For Desktop (Web Interface):

1. **Go to your SharePoint site** and navigate to the document library or list where you want to set permissions.
2. Click on the **Settings gear** icon in the top-right corner, then select **Site Settings**.
3. Under the **Users and Permissions** section, click on **Site Permissions**.

4. You will see a list of existing groups and users with their permission levels. Click on the **Grant Permissions** button to assign permissions to a new user or group.
5. In the pop-up window, type the **names or email addresses** of the users or groups you want to add.
6. Choose the **permission level** for the users, such as **Read**, **Contribute**, or **Full Control**.
7. Click **Share** to apply the permissions.

To **break inheritance** and assign unique permissions to a specific document library:

1. In the document library, click on the **Library Settings** option (or **List Settings** for lists).
2. Under **Permissions and Management**, click **Permissions for this document library**.
3. Click **Stop Inheriting Permissions** to break inheritance from the site-level permissions.
4. Now you can customize permissions for this library by clicking **Grant Permissions** or modifying existing permissions.

For Mobile Devices (iOS/Android):

1. Open the **SharePoint app** and navigate to the site or document library where you want to set permissions.
2. Tap the **three-dot menu** next to the document or folder, then select **Manage Access**.
3. From here, you can add users, assign permissions, or change the access level.

4. To break inheritance or modify permissions for specific users, you may need to use the web or desktop app, as these options may be limited in the mobile interface.

3. Managing Access to Document Libraries

Managing access to document libraries ensures that only authorized users can view or edit your files. It's important to control access at the library level, especially when dealing with sensitive information.

For Desktop (Web Interface):

1. In your SharePoint site, navigate to the document library where you want to manage access.
2. Click on the **Settings gear** icon and select **Library Settings**.
3. Under **Permissions and Management**, click on **Permissions for this document library**.

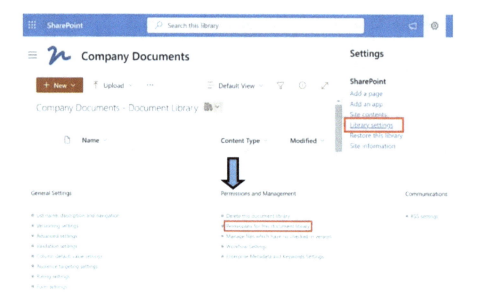

4. If you want to change permissions for a specific group or user, click on their name and then **Edit User Permissions**.
5. Select the new permission level you want to assign (e.g., **Read**, **Contribute**, or **Full Control**).

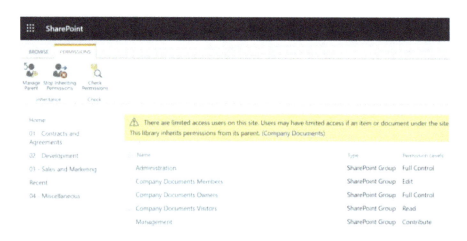

6. If you want to stop inheriting permissions from the site, click **Stop Inheriting Permissions**, and then you can assign custom permissions for this library.
7. You can also **remove permissions** for users who no longer need access.

For Mobile Devices (iOS/Android):

1. Open the **SharePoint app** and navigate to the document library.
2. Tap the **three-dot menu** and select **Manage Access**.
3. You can grant, modify, or revoke permissions for users directly from this menu.
4. Advanced options like **breaking inheritance** and **setting unique permissions** are typically not available on mobile devices. Use the desktop or web version for more complex permission management.

4. Understanding SharePoint Groups and Roles

SharePoint groups and roles play a crucial role in simplifying permission management by grouping users with similar access needs. Assigning roles to groups ensures that permissions are consistent across a site.

Creating and Managing SharePoint Groups:

1. In your **SharePoint site**, click the **Settings gear** and select **Site Settings**.
2. Under **Users and Permissions**, click on **Site Permissions**.

3. On the Permissions page, click on **Create Group** to create a new SharePoint group.
4. Name the group and set the **permission level** (e.g., **Contribute** or **Edit**).
5. You can add users to the group from here by typing their names or email addresses.
6. Once the group is created, users will have the permissions assigned to that group.

Assigning Roles to Groups:

1. Go to **Site Permissions**.
2. Select the **group** you want to assign roles to.
3. Click **Edit User Permissions** and choose a permission level based on the group's needs.
4. SharePoint roles such as **Owners**, **Members**, and **Visitors** are pre-defined and offer varying levels of access. You can assign users to these roles when creating a group.

Best Practices for Managing Permissions:

- **Use Groups**: Instead of assigning permissions individually, create groups for different roles (e.g., HR, Marketing, Management) and assign permissions to the group. This simplifies managing permissions as your team grows.
- **Limit External Sharing**: When sharing documents externally, set specific permissions for external users, and ensure you are following your organization's security policies.

- **Review Permissions Regularly**: Periodically review who has access to your SharePoint sites and document libraries to ensure permissions remain aligned with user needs.

Chapter 15: Sharing and Collaborating in SharePoint

Sharepoint is designed for collaboration, allowing teams to work together on documents and projects efficiently. This chapter covers the various ways you can share and collaborate on content in SharePoint, whether it's with internal team members or external partners.

1. Sharing Documents and Folders in SharePoint

One of the key benefits of SharePoint is the ability to share documents and folders with others for collaboration. You can control who has access to your content and what actions they can perform, such as viewing, editing, or sharing further.

For Desktop (Web Interface):

1. **Navigate to Your SharePoint Site** and go to the document library where your file or folder is located.
2. **Select the File or Folder** you want to share by clicking the checkbox next to it.
3. Click the **Share** button located in the toolbar at the top of the page.
4. A pop-up window will appear with sharing options. Here, you can:
   - **Invite People**: Type the names or email addresses of the people you want to share with.

- Set Permissions: Choose whether the people you're sharing with can **View** or **Edit** the content.
  - You can also click on **Anyone with the link, People in your organization,** or **Specific people** to adjust access levels.
5. After setting permissions, click **Send** to share the document or folder.

For Mobile Devices (iOS/Android):

1. Open the **SharePoint app** and navigate to the document or folder you want to share.
2. Tap the **three-dot menu** next to the item, then select **Share**.
3. Enter the names or email addresses of the people you want to share the content with.
4. Adjust the permissions (view or edit) and then tap **Send** to share the link.

2. Inviting External Users to SharePoint

Sometimes, you need to share content with people outside your organization, such as clients, vendors, or collaborators. SharePoint makes it easy to invite external users while giving you full control over their access permissions.

For Desktop (Web Interface):

1. **Select the File or Folder** you want to share with external users.
2. Click the **Share** button in the toolbar.

3. In the pop-up window, click on **Anyone with the link** or **Specific people** to allow external access.
   - ○ **Anyone with the link**: The link can be shared freely, and anyone with the link can access the document, depending on the permissions you set.
   - ○ **Specific people**: Only the people you invite via email can access the content. They'll need to verify their identity before accessing the document.
4. Type the email addresses of the external users you want to invite.
5. Choose their permission level (View or Edit) and click **Send** to invite them.

For Mobile Devices (iOS/Android):

1. Open the **SharePoint app** and navigate to the file or folder you wish to share.
2. Tap the **three-dot menu** next to the item and select **Share**.
3. Tap on **Anyone with the link** or **Specific people**.
4. Enter the email addresses of the external users and set the permissions.
5. Tap **Send** to share the file or folder with external users.

Note: External sharing must be enabled in your SharePoint settings. If you do not see the external sharing options, contact your SharePoint admin.

3. Setting Permissions for Shared Content

When sharing documents or folders in SharePoint, it's crucial to set the appropriate permissions to control who can view or edit the content. You can modify permissions for individual users or for everyone with the link.

For Desktop (Web Interface):

1. Select the file or folder you want to manage permissions for, then click the **three-dot menu** and select **Manage Access**.
2. You'll see a list of users and groups who have access to the document. To adjust permissions:
   - o Click on the **Drop-down menu** next to the user's name.
   - o Choose **Can Edit** or **Can View** to set the desired permission level.
   - o To remove access entirely, click **Remove** next to the user's name.
3. If you want to restrict access further, click on **Advanced** to go to the permissions settings page, where you can stop inheriting permissions from the parent site and set custom permissions for the specific document or folder.

For Mobile Devices (iOS/Android):

1. In the **SharePoint app**, select the file or folder you want to adjust permissions for.
2. Tap the **three-dot menu** next to the item and select **Manage Access**.
3. From here, you can change the permissions for users, such as toggling between **Can Edit** or **Can View**.
4. Tap **Done** to save your changes.

4. Collaboration Features: Comments, Alerts, and Notifications

SharePoint offers several powerful collaboration tools to streamline communication and ensure that everyone stays on the same page when working on documents or projects.

Comments:

SharePoint allows users to add comments directly to documents, making it easier to provide feedback, ask questions, or discuss changes.

For Desktop (Web Interface):

1. Open the document in **Edit Mode** by clicking on the file.
2. In the document, navigate to the **Comments section** (usually in the right-hand pane).
3. Type your comment in the text box and click **Post** to share it with other collaborators.
4. You can also reply to existing comments by clicking on them and typing your response.

For Mobile Devices (iOS/Android):

1. Open the document in **Edit Mode**.
2. Scroll to the **Comments section** and tap to add a comment.
3. Type your comment and tap **Post** to share.
4. You can also reply to others' comments in the same way.

Alerts:

SharePoint provides a way to stay informed of any changes made to documents or libraries by setting up **alerts**. This ensures you are notified of important updates.

For Desktop (Web Interface):

1. Navigate to the document library or file you want to set an alert for.
2. Click on the **three-dot menu** next to the file or library and select **Alert Me**.

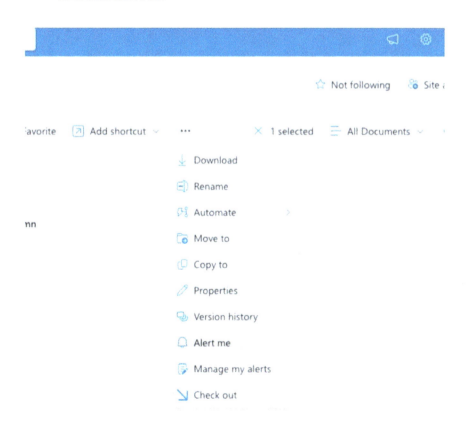

3. In the Alert settings window, choose the type of alert you want (e.g., **All changes**, **New items added**, etc.).
4. Select how you would like to be notified (e.g., **Email** or **Text**), and click **OK**.

For Mobile Devices (iOS/Android):

1. In the **SharePoint app**, navigate to the document or folder you want to set an alert for.
2. Tap the **three-dot menu** and select **Alert Me**.
3. Choose the type of alert and the notification method.
4. Tap **OK** to confirm your settings.

Notifications:

Notifications keep you updated on recent activities within SharePoint, such as file edits, document sharing, and comments.

- **Document Notifications**: Whenever someone comments, edits, or shares a document, you'll receive a notification.
- **Site Notifications**: Get notifications about changes made to SharePoint sites, including new document uploads or permissions updates.

You can manage notifications in **Site Settings** under **Site Permissions**, where you can enable or disable email and push notifications.

Best Practices for Sharing and Collaborating:

- **Use Comments for Feedback**: Always use SharePoint's built-in commenting features rather than emailing feedback. This keeps all communication within the context of the document.
- **Set Alerts**: Set alerts for documents you frequently collaborate on to stay updated on any changes in real-time.
- **Control External Access**: Only share documents externally when necessary. Regularly review the people who have access to external links and remove any that are no longer needed.
- **Encourage Co-Authoring**: SharePoint works seamlessly with Microsoft Office apps, enabling co-authoring. Encourage real-time collaboration on documents to increase productivity.

Chapter 16: Using SharePoint Lists

SharePoint Lists are a versatile tool for managing and organizing data within SharePoint. They allow you to store a variety of content types, such as tasks, contacts, links, and other types of structured information, all in one place. This chapter will cover everything you need to know about creating, managing, and customizing SharePoint Lists.

1. What Are SharePoint Lists?

SharePoint Lists are essentially a collection of data organized into rows and columns, similar to a spreadsheet. Each row represents a list item, and each column represents a property or field of that item. They allow for the easy management of data and can be customized to fit various business needs.

You can use SharePoint Lists for:

- **Tracking Tasks**: A list to keep track of tasks and their status.
- **Managing Contacts**: A list of people, their details, and any relevant information.
- **Storing Inventory**: A list for tracking items, quantities, and locations.
- **Custom Data Types**: Lists for anything your team needs to track or manage.

Key Features of SharePoint Lists:

- **Structured Data**: Lists are designed to store data in a structured format.
- **Customizable Views**: You can change the way your list appears based on the data you're working with.
- **Integration with Other SharePoint Features**: Lists can be connected with workflows, document libraries, and other SharePoint components for a more dynamic experience.

2. Creating and Managing Lists in SharePoint

Creating a list in SharePoint is simple and can be done in a few steps. You can also manage your lists to add columns, modify data types, and set permissions.

For Desktop (Web Interface):

1. **Navigate to Your SharePoint Site** and go to the location where you want to create a list (e.g., a specific site or library).
2. On the **home page** of the site, click on the **Settings Gear** in the top-right corner and choose **Site Contents**.
3. Click **New** at the top of the Site Contents page, then select **List**.
4. You'll be prompted to choose from a variety of templates, such as Task List, Contacts List, or Custom List. Choose one that fits your needs or select **Custom List** to start from scratch.
5. Give your list a **name** and description. Click **Create** to finish.

Managing Lists:

- **Accessing a List**: Once created, you can access your list from the **Site Contents** page or the navigation menu of the site.
- **Editing List Settings**: To modify a list's settings (e.g., permissions, columns, or views), click the **Settings Gear** again and select **List Settings**.
- **Permissions**: You can set permissions for individual users or groups, allowing you to control who can view or edit the list.

For Mobile Devices (iOS/Android):

1. Open the **SharePoint app** and go to your site.
2. Tap **Site Contents**, then tap the **+ icon** to create a new list.
3. Select the type of list you want to create and name it. Once done, tap **Create**.

3. Adding, Editing, and Deleting List Items

Once your list is created, you'll need to know how to add, edit, and delete list items. These are the core actions you'll perform regularly in SharePoint Lists.

For Desktop (Web Interface):

- **Adding Items**: To add a new item to the list, click on **New** at the top of the list. A form will appear where you can input data for the columns defined in the list.
  - ○ Fill out the fields with the required information, then click **Save** to add the item.

- **Editing Items**: To edit an existing item, click on the **three-dot menu** next to the item, then select **Edit**. Update the fields and click **Save** to apply the changes.
- **Deleting Items**: To delete an item, click the **three-dot menu** next to the item, and select **Delete**. You will be asked to confirm the deletion.

For Mobile Devices (iOS/Android):

- **Adding Items**: In the **SharePoint app**, open the list and tap the **+ icon** to add a new item. Fill out the form and tap **Save** to add it.
- **Editing Items**: Tap on an existing item in the list to open it, then tap **Edit**. After making the changes, tap **Save** to update the item.
- **Deleting Items**: Tap the **three-dot menu** next to an item and select **Delete**.

4. Customizing List Views and Columns

One of the most powerful features of SharePoint Lists is the ability to customize how the list is displayed. You can adjust the layout, add columns, and filter data to focus on what matters most.

Customizing Columns:

Columns in SharePoint Lists define the data types for each field. You can add or remove columns, change column types, and apply different settings for how data is displayed.

1. **Navigate to the List** and click the **Settings Gear**, then select **List Settings**.

2. In the **Columns** section, click on **Create Column** to add a new column to the list.
3. Choose a column type (e.g., Single line of text, Choice, Number, Date and Time, etc.).
4. Fill out the settings for the new column and click **OK** to add it to the list.

Customizing Views:

Views allow you to display data in different formats, like a standard list, calendar, or Gantt chart, depending on what makes sense for your data.

1. In the list settings, under the **Views** section, click on **Create View**.
2. Choose a view type (e.g., Standard View, Calendar View, or Datasheet View).
3. Customize the view by selecting which columns to display, sorting the list, and applying filters.
4. Click **OK** to save the view. You can switch between views from the list's toolbar at any time.

For Mobile Devices (iOS/Android):

- **Customizing Columns**: In the **SharePoint app**, tap the **three-dot menu** on the list and choose **Settings** to add or modify columns.
- **Customizing Views**: To filter or change views, tap the **filter icon** at the top of the list to adjust how the data is displayed.

Best Practices for Using SharePoint Lists:

- **Use Columns Wisely**: Be mindful of how many columns you create. Too many can clutter the view and confuse users.
- **Leverage Views**: Create multiple views to display data in different formats, depending on user needs. For example, one view could show completed tasks, while another shows tasks in progress.
- **Set Permissions Carefully**: When managing sensitive data, make sure only the appropriate people have access to the list and set permissions accordingly.
- **Regularly Clean Up Lists**: Archive or delete old list items that are no longer necessary to keep the list clean and manageable.

Chapter 17: Automating Tasks with Workflows

Sharepoint workflows allow you to automate routine tasks, reducing manual effort and improving efficiency within teams. In this chapter, we will explore how SharePoint workflows work, how to create and manage them, and how to use Power Automate to extend workflow capabilities.

1. Introduction to SharePoint Workflows

A **workflow** in SharePoint is a set of automated actions or tasks that are executed based on certain triggers or conditions. Workflows can help streamline and automate processes like document approval, task tracking, or notification sending, ensuring consistency and efficiency across your organization.

Why Use Workflows in SharePoint?

- **Efficiency**: Reduce the time spent on repetitive tasks.
- **Consistency**: Ensure tasks are performed in a standardized way every time.
- **Collaboration**: Enable better teamwork by automating approvals and task assignments.
- **Error Reduction**: Minimize the risk of human error by automating processes.

There are two main types of workflows:

- **SharePoint Designer Workflows**: These were traditionally used in SharePoint on-premises environments but have now been phased out for cloud-based environments like SharePoint Online.
- **Power Automate (formerly Microsoft Flow)**: This is the modern tool for creating workflows that can integrate SharePoint with various Microsoft 365 apps and external services.

2. Creating and Managing Basic Workflows

Creating workflows in SharePoint is a straightforward process that allows you to automate common actions, such as document approval or task assignment.

For SharePoint Online (using Power Automate):

1. **Access Power Automate**: In your SharePoint site, click on **Automate** in the top menu or use the **Power Automate** app.
2. **Create a New Flow**:
   o In Power Automate, click on **Create** and select **Automated Flow** or **Instant Flow**.
   o Choose a **trigger** for the workflow (e.g., when a new item is created, when a document is approved, etc.).
   o Define the **actions** that should occur when the trigger happens (e.g., send an email, update a list item, etc.).
3. **Customize the Flow**:
   o Select actions like **Send an Email, Start an Approval Process, Create Item in Another List**, and more.

- Configure the parameters for each action, such as the recipient of an email or the type of approval workflow needed.
4. **Save and Test the Flow**:
   - After setting up the workflow, click **Save** and test it by performing the trigger action.
   - Monitor the flow's execution through the Power Automate portal, where you can track its success or failure and make necessary adjustments.

Managing Workflows:

- **View Flow History**: In Power Automate, click on **My Flows** to view and manage your active flows.
- **Edit Flows**: If you need to make adjustments, click on a flow and select **Edit** to update triggers or actions.
- **Delete Flows**: To remove a flow, simply click the **three-dot menu** and select **Delete**.

3. Automating Processes with Power Automate

Power Automate is a robust tool for automating workflows across SharePoint and other Microsoft 365 services, such as Outlook, Teams, and Planner. This section will cover more advanced uses for Power Automate.

Advanced Power Automate Scenarios:

- **Automated Document Approval**:
  - Set up a flow where, once a document is uploaded to a SharePoint document library, an approval request

is automatically sent to a designated person. If approved, the document is moved to a designated folder, and a notification is sent to the author.
- **Task Assignment and Notification**:
  - o Automate the process of assigning tasks in Microsoft Planner when a new SharePoint list item is created. The assigned user will receive an email with task details.
- **Data Synchronization**:
  - o Set up a flow that automatically syncs data between SharePoint lists and external services, such as creating records in a CRM or sending form data to another platform.

Using Templates:

- Power Automate provides various pre-built **templates** for common workflows. These templates can be customized based on your organization's needs. Examples include:
  - o Approval workflows
  - o Notifications for new documents
  - o Automated reports

  To access templates:

  - o Go to **Power Automate** and select **Templates**. Browse the catalog or search for templates based on the type of workflow you want to create.

4. Best Practices for SharePoint Workflows

When working with workflows, it's essential to follow best practices to ensure they are efficient, easy to manage, and do not cause performance issues.

Best Practices:

- **Define Clear Workflow Objectives**: Before creating a workflow, clearly define the process it will automate. Identify the trigger, actions, and expected outcome.
- **Keep Workflows Simple**: Avoid creating overly complex workflows that can be difficult to manage. Break large workflows into smaller, more manageable flows if necessary.
- **Test Before Deployment**: Always test workflows in a development or sandbox environment before rolling them out to production. This ensures that everything works as expected and reduces the risk of errors.
- **Monitor Workflow Performance**: Regularly check the performance of your workflows. Power Automate provides analytics to help you identify failed flows and optimize them.
- **Use Conditional Logic Wisely**: Conditional logic (e.g., if/else statements) can help create flexible workflows, but overusing it can complicate your flow. Use it only when necessary.
- **Document Workflow Processes**: Keep a record of the workflows you've created, including their purpose and logic. This will help future administrators understand the flow and make updates if needed.

Common Workflow Pitfalls to Avoid:

- **Long-Running Workflows**: Long workflows can consume excessive resources and slow down performance. Break down long processes into smaller stages if possible.
- **Lack of Error Handling**: Always include error handling steps (e.g., sending an alert if a workflow fails). This will help you quickly address any issues.
- **Overcomplicating the Workflow**: Adding too many actions can lead to a complex, hard-to-maintain workflow. Start with simple actions and build on them gradually.

Chapter 18: Advanced SharePoint Features

his chapter dives into the advanced features of SharePoint that can help you further customize and streamline your SharePoint environment. We will cover how to create custom forms, integrate SharePoint with Microsoft Teams, manage site collections, and leverage Power Apps to extend SharePoint's functionality.

1. Creating Custom SharePoint Forms

Custom forms are a powerful way to collect and display data on your SharePoint sites. These forms allow you to tailor data collection to suit your needs, creating a more intuitive and streamlined process for users.

How to Create Custom Forms in SharePoint:

1. **Using SharePoint Lists to Create Forms:**
   - Navigate to the **SharePoint site** where you want to add a custom form.
   - Select the **List** or **Library** where you want the form to appear.
   - Click on **New** to open the default form.
   - Instead of using the default form, click on **Integrate** and then select **Power Apps** to open the form creation interface.

- In **Power Apps**, you can fully customize the form, adding new fields, adjusting the layout, and incorporating conditional logic.
- After designing your form, click **Save** and **Publish** to make it available for use.

2. **Using InfoPath (for legacy SharePoint environments)**:
   - InfoPath is a deprecated tool but may still be used in older SharePoint environments. To create a custom form:
     - Open **InfoPath** and design your form by dragging fields from your SharePoint list.
     - Publish the form to your SharePoint site, and link it to the list or library.
     - While InfoPath is no longer actively supported in SharePoint Online, some organizations continue to use it.

Customizing Forms in Power Apps:

Power Apps is the modern tool for creating dynamic and responsive forms in SharePoint. Here are some key features you can leverage:

- **Custom Layouts**: Choose from various templates or create a layout from scratch.
- **Conditional Formatting**: Display certain fields based on user input.
- **Business Logic**: Implement logic such as calculating totals or validating data.

2. Integrating SharePoint with Microsoft Teams

Integrating SharePoint with Microsoft Teams creates a seamless collaboration environment. By connecting SharePoint libraries and lists to Teams, users can access, edit, and share content directly from Teams.

How to Integrate SharePoint with Microsoft Teams:

1. **Adding SharePoint Document Libraries to Teams**:
   - o Open **Microsoft Teams** and navigate to the channel where you want to add the SharePoint document library.
   - o Click on the **+** icon (Add a tab) at the top of the channel.
   - o Select **SharePoint** from the list of available apps.
   - o You can now link to a specific SharePoint document library, list, or site. This allows you to access and edit SharePoint documents directly within the Teams interface.
2. **Using SharePoint Lists in Teams**:
   - o In the same way, you can add a SharePoint **list** to a channel in Teams.
   - o Click the **+** icon, choose **SharePoint**, and then select the relevant list from the SharePoint site.
   - o This integration allows team members to interact with SharePoint lists without leaving the Teams environment.
3. **Using the SharePoint Connector in Teams**:

- o You can set up alerts and notifications from SharePoint to Teams using the **SharePoint Connector**.
- o In Teams, go to the desired channel and click on **Connectors**.
- o Add the **SharePoint Connector** to the channel to receive alerts whenever content changes or when new items are added to a SharePoint list.

3. Managing Site Collections

Site collections are containers for SharePoint sites, providing a hierarchical structure for organizing content. Managing site collections involves organizing them efficiently, ensuring proper access permissions, and maintaining scalability.

How to Manage Site Collections:

1. **Creating a Site Collection**:
   - o Go to **SharePoint Admin Center** by navigating to **admin.microsoft.com**.
   - o Under the **Sites** section, click on **Active sites**.
   - o Select **Create** and choose the type of site you want to create (e.g., Team Site or Communication Site).
   - o Provide a name, description, and site collection URL.
   - o Choose the primary administrator and configure storage options.
   - o Click **Finish** to create the site collection.
2. **Managing Permissions for Site Collections**:

- o Site collections typically have a **Site Collection Administrator**, which has full control over all sites within the collection.
- o From the **SharePoint Admin Center**, you can assign permissions to site collections, giving users the ability to manage site collections or view them.
- o You can also assign permissions at a more granular level to specific sites within the collection.
3. **Managing Storage for Site Collections**:
- o Site collections come with a predefined storage quota, which can be adjusted if necessary.
- o In the **SharePoint Admin Center**, under the **Sites** tab, you can view usage and adjust storage limits for your site collections.
4. **Accessing and Managing Subsites**:
- o Within a site collection, you can create subsites that are independent but still linked to the parent site collection. Manage the permissions and settings for subsites individually.

4. Using Power Apps with SharePoint

Power Apps is a powerful tool that can be integrated with SharePoint to create custom apps and workflows that extend SharePoint's functionality. By using Power Apps with SharePoint, you can create custom forms, automate business processes, and even build standalone applications.

Integrating Power Apps with SharePoint:

1. **Creating Custom SharePoint Apps**:

- In **SharePoint**, open the **List** or **Document Library** where you want to use Power Apps.
- Click on **Power Apps** in the command bar, then select **Create an App**.
- Power Apps will open, where you can customize the app's appearance and functionality, and configure it to interact with your SharePoint data.

2. **Customizing SharePoint Lists with Power Apps**:
   - Once in Power Apps, customize the list form with elements such as dropdowns, checkboxes, and buttons.
   - Add logic to interact with your list data, for example, by submitting data or triggering workflows.

3. **Connecting Power Apps to Other Data Sources**:
   - Power Apps supports integration with other data sources beyond SharePoint, such as **SQL Server**, **Dynamics 365**, and **Office 365** apps.
   - You can create apps that pull data from multiple sources and display it in a single interface.

4. **Embedding Power Apps in SharePoint**:
   - Once your Power App is ready, you can embed it directly into a SharePoint page using the **Power Apps web part**.
   - This allows users to interact with the app directly within the SharePoint interface, creating a seamless experience.

Part III: OneDrive and SharePoint Together

Chapter 19: OneDrive and SharePoint Integration

I n this chapter, we explore the seamless integration between OneDrive and SharePoint. Understanding how these two services work together is essential for optimizing your file storage, access, and collaboration. We'll dive into syncing document libraries, accessing SharePoint files via OneDrive, and how co-authoring features allow real-time collaboration on shared documents.

1. How OneDrive and SharePoint Work Together

OneDrive and SharePoint are both part of the Microsoft 365 ecosystem, designed to enhance productivity, collaboration, and file management. While they each serve distinct purposes, they are closely integrated to provide a cohesive experience.

Key Differences Between OneDrive and SharePoint:

- **OneDrive** is primarily a personal cloud storage solution, used for storing individual files and documents.
- **SharePoint** is a collaboration platform designed for managing content, knowledge, and applications within a team or organization.

Despite these differences, OneDrive and SharePoint work in tandem:

- **OneDrive** is often used for individual file storage, but it can also be used to sync SharePoint libraries for offline access.
- **SharePoint** is used for team and organization-wide content management, and users can access SharePoint libraries through OneDrive for easy collaboration and file management.

By syncing SharePoint libraries with OneDrive, users gain the flexibility to manage and access shared team files as if they were stored locally, while still maintaining all the collaboration and version control features of SharePoint.

2. Syncing SharePoint Document Libraries with OneDrive

One of the key features of integrating OneDrive with SharePoint is the ability to sync SharePoint document libraries to your OneDrive for offline access. This allows you to work on files stored in SharePoint, even when you are not connected to the internet.

How to Sync SharePoint Document Libraries with OneDrive:

1. **Navigate to the SharePoint Site**:
   - Go to the **SharePoint document library** you want to sync.
   - Ensure you are logged into Microsoft 365 and have access to the SharePoint site.
2. **Sync the Library**:
   - On the document library page, click the **Sync** button at the top of the page (it may also appear under the "Documents" tab).

- o If you haven't set up OneDrive yet, you'll be prompted to install the OneDrive sync app.
- o Once the sync app is installed, the library will be added to your **OneDrive** folder on your computer.
3. **Access Synced Files Locally**:
    - o After syncing, you can access the SharePoint files directly from your local **OneDrive folder** on your computer, just like any other file.
    - o Files and folders will automatically sync between your computer and SharePoint whenever you are connected to the internet.
4. **Sync Multiple Libraries**:
    - o You can sync multiple SharePoint libraries to your OneDrive by repeating the process for each library you want to sync.

Managing Sync Settings:

You can manage syncing settings through the **OneDrive settings** by clicking the OneDrive icon in the system tray and selecting **Settings**. From here, you can manage which libraries to sync, whether to sync all files or select specific folders, and troubleshoot syncing issues.

3. Accessing SharePoint Files via OneDrive

Once SharePoint libraries are synced to OneDrive, users can access SharePoint files from the OneDrive app on desktop or mobile devices. This provides a unified location for managing both personal files stored in OneDrive and team files stored in SharePoint.

How to Access SharePoint Files via OneDrive:

1. **On Desktop**:
   - Open the **OneDrive** folder on your computer.
   - You will see folders for your personal files and synced SharePoint libraries.
   - Navigate through the folders to find and access your SharePoint files as if they were stored locally.
2. **On Mobile Devices (iOS & Android)**:
   - Open the **OneDrive** app on your mobile device.
   - In the app, you will see **Personal** and **Shared** sections.
   - Under **Shared**, you can find the SharePoint libraries you've synced and access their contents.

Accessing Files Without an Internet Connection:

- When files are synced to your OneDrive, they are available for offline access. If you're working on a file offline, once you reconnect to the internet, any changes will sync automatically with SharePoint.

4. Co-authoring Documents Stored in SharePoint Using OneDrive

One of the standout features of both OneDrive and SharePoint is their real-time collaboration capabilities. You can co-author documents that are stored in SharePoint, using OneDrive as the interface for managing and editing these documents.

How to Co-author Documents in SharePoint Using Onedrive:

1. **Open a Shared Document**:
   - o Navigate to the SharePoint document library (via OneDrive or SharePoint itself) and open the document you want to edit.
   - o You can open documents directly in **Microsoft 365 apps** like Word, Excel, or PowerPoint.
2. **Collaborate in Real-Time**:
   - o Once the document is open, you and other collaborators can edit the document simultaneously.
   - o You will see the changes made by other people in real-time, as well as any comments or suggestions.
   - o The co-authors' names will appear alongside the text or cells they are editing, and each change will be marked with a different color.
3. **Version History**:
   - o Both OneDrive and SharePoint keep track of the document's **version history**. You can see who made which changes and revert to earlier versions if necessary.
4. **Adding Comments**:
   - o Collaborators can leave comments and feedback directly within the document. These comments can be resolved when the necessary changes have been made.
5. **Notifications**:
   - o You can set up **notifications** to alert you when someone else has edited the document. This feature ensures that you're always up to date with any changes made by other collaborators.

Chapter 20: Cross-Platform Collaboration

I n today's fast-paced, mobile-first world, the ability to seamlessly collaborate across different devices is crucial. Both **OneDrive** and **SharePoint** are designed to offer smooth collaboration experiences across platforms—whether on desktop, mobile, or the web. This chapter will guide you through using both tools across multiple devices and provide tips for working offline.

1. Using OneDrive and SharePoint on Desktop, Mobile, and Web

Both **OneDrive** and **SharePoint** offer intuitive interfaces and functionality across multiple platforms. This flexibility ensures you can access, edit, and collaborate on files no matter where you are or what device you are using.

On Desktop:

- **OneDrive**: When installed on your desktop, OneDrive creates a folder on your local computer, allowing you to work directly with your files while keeping them synced to the cloud. Files are accessible through **File Explorer** (Windows) or **Finder** (Mac).
- **SharePoint**: Access SharePoint sites and document libraries via your desktop browser (Edge, Chrome, etc.) or directly

through Microsoft apps (Word, Excel, PowerPoint) when working on documents stored in SharePoint.

On Mobile:

- **OneDrive App**: The OneDrive mobile app allows you to access files stored in OneDrive and any synced SharePoint libraries. The app provides a streamlined interface for managing documents, photos, and videos, even allowing you to scan and upload files directly from your phone.
- **SharePoint App**: The SharePoint app for mobile enables you to access SharePoint sites, documents, and news on the go. It's designed for easy navigation and collaboration, giving you access to team sites and files stored in SharePoint.

On the Web:

- **OneDrive Web**: OneDrive's web interface is perfect for accessing your files from any device with internet access. The **OneDrive website** offers full functionality, including file management, sharing, and editing using **Microsoft Office for the web**.
- **SharePoint Web**: The SharePoint web interface allows users to navigate and manage document libraries, sites, and lists. You can view and edit documents directly in the browser, collaborate in real-time, and access your entire SharePoint ecosystem.

2. Collaborating on Files Across Devices

One of the most significant benefits of OneDrive and SharePoint is their **cross-device collaboration capabilities**. Whether you're at the office, on the go, or working from home, you can collaborate in real time across devices and platforms.

Co-Authoring Documents:

- **Real-Time Editing**: No matter if you're using a desktop, mobile device, or the web, OneDrive and SharePoint support real-time co-authoring. When you and your team members edit the same document, changes are instantly reflected across all devices. This ensures that everyone is working with the most up-to-date version of the file.
- **Notifications**: As collaborators make changes, notifications can be sent to keep everyone updated. This is especially useful when working across devices to ensure smooth communication and collaboration.

Accessing Files on Multiple Devices:

- Files stored in **OneDrive** and **SharePoint** are automatically available across your devices. You can start working on a file on your desktop, edit it on your phone while commuting, and finish it up on your laptop once you're back at your desk.
- You can also switch between **Microsoft Office apps**, such as Word, Excel, and PowerPoint, across platforms without losing formatting or features. The seamless integration between OneDrive, SharePoint, and Office ensures that your

documents remain consistent no matter where you access them.

Document Comments and Feedback:

- Adding comments, making edits, or suggesting changes is easy on both mobile and desktop. All feedback is visible across devices, ensuring everyone stays on the same page. On the web and mobile apps, you can also use @mentions to tag collaborators in comments or notifications.

3. Using SharePoint and OneDrive Offline

Working without an internet connection doesn't mean you have to stop collaborating or editing files. OneDrive and SharePoint offer **offline capabilities**, allowing you to access and work on your files even when you are not connected to the internet.

Offline Access with OneDrive:

- **Sync Files for Offline Access**: Files in OneDrive can be marked for offline access. Once you've synced your files to your computer, you can open and edit them even when there's no internet connection. These changes will automatically sync to the cloud once you reconnect.
- **Mobile Offline Access**: In the **OneDrive mobile app**, you can choose specific files and folders to be available offline. This is especially useful when traveling or in places with unreliable internet access. The app will sync files back to the cloud once the device is online.

Offline Access with SharePoint:

- **Sync SharePoint Libraries**: Just like OneDrive, SharePoint libraries can be synced to your device. By syncing document libraries with OneDrive, you can work on documents stored in SharePoint offline. When you regain internet access, the changes are synced to SharePoint.
- **Accessing SharePoint Files on Mobile**: On mobile devices, the **SharePoint mobile app** allows you to view files offline. While editing offline is not as seamless as with OneDrive, you can still view documents and make minor changes. Once online, your updates will sync with SharePoint.

Chapter 21: Advanced Collaboration Tools

In this chapter, we will explore **advanced collaboration tools** available in **OneDrive** and **SharePoint**. These tools integrate seamlessly with other **Microsoft 365** applications like **Teams**, **Planner**, and **To-Do** to enhance team productivity, streamline project management, and improve collaborative workflows. Let's delve into how you can use these tools to take your collaboration efforts to the next level.

1. Microsoft Teams Integration with SharePoint and OneDrive

Microsoft Teams is at the heart of collaboration in the modern workplace. Teams integrate seamlessly with both **OneDrive** and **SharePoint**, providing a hub for communication, file sharing, and real-time collaboration.

Using Teams with OneDrive:

- **File Sharing**: You can share files directly from OneDrive to Teams by attaching them to chat conversations or channels. Files uploaded to OneDrive are accessible through the **Files** tab in Teams, and any changes are synced automatically.
- **Collaborating on OneDrive Files**: When you collaborate on a document stored in OneDrive via Teams, you can work together in real-time using the **Microsoft Office apps**.

Everyone can see changes live, enhancing efficiency during team discussions or meetings.

Using Teams with SharePoint:

- **Accessing SharePoint Sites and Libraries in Teams**: SharePoint sites can be added as **tabs** in Teams channels, making it easy for team members to access shared document libraries and project-specific files.
- **Co-Authoring Documents in SharePoint**: When files stored in SharePoint are opened through Teams, you can collaborate on documents in real-time using the **Office apps**, just like in Teams or OneDrive.

File Permissions and SharePoint Integration:

- **Permissions**: Teams respects the permissions set in SharePoint. When you share files from SharePoint within Teams, the permissions you set in SharePoint—whether it's view-only, edit, or full control—are maintained.
- **Automated Document Management**: With SharePoint's robust document management features, you can automate the creation, categorization, and sharing of documents directly from within Teams.

2. Using Planner and To-Do with SharePoint

Microsoft Planner and **To-Do** are both powerful task management tools that integrate seamlessly with SharePoint and OneDrive, making them excellent choices for organizing and tracking tasks, especially in team environments.

Using Planner with SharePoint:

- **Planner and SharePoint Site Integration**: You can add a **Planner board** as a tab to your SharePoint site. This allows your team to track tasks, assign responsibilities, and set deadlines directly within the SharePoint site.
- **Task Management within SharePoint**: You can use **Planner** to organize tasks related to a specific project, linking them directly to documents or project files stored in SharePoint. As tasks are updated, the Planner board is automatically updated, keeping everything synchronized.

Using To-Do with SharePoint:

- **Task Lists in SharePoint**: SharePoint's task list feature can be connected to **Microsoft To-Do**, enabling you to manage personal tasks, reminders, and follow-up actions related to the documents and projects stored in SharePoint.
- **Personal Task Management**: While Planner is designed for team tasks, **To-Do** is great for personal task management. You can use **To-Do** alongside SharePoint to manage your individual tasks related to SharePoint files or team projects. Tasks from **Planner** will automatically show up in **To-Do** to help you stay on top of everything.

3. Real-Time Co-Authoring with Office Apps

Real-time co-authoring is a core feature when working with **Microsoft Office apps** (Word, Excel, PowerPoint) and it extends across both **OneDrive** and **SharePoint**. This feature allows multiple users to work on the same document at the same time, making collaboration more dynamic and efficient.

Co-Authoring in OneDrive:

- **Real-Time Collaboration**: When you share documents from **OneDrive**, collaborators can edit them simultaneously, seeing each other's changes as they happen. This works on desktop, web, and mobile versions of **Word**, **Excel**, and **PowerPoint**.
- **Tracking Changes**: As you co-author, the document will show **who** made which changes, and collaborators can leave comments for further feedback or clarification.

Co-Authoring in SharePoint:

- **Using SharePoint for Team Collaboration**: SharePoint allows the same real-time collaboration functionality as OneDrive. Since SharePoint is designed for team-based work, it makes sense to use it as a centralized platform for co-authoring documents in real-time with colleagues.
- **Accessing Files for Co-Authoring**: Files stored in SharePoint can be edited simultaneously by multiple team members using Office apps, either in the **SharePoint web app**, desktop version of Office apps, or mobile devices.

4. Using SharePoint and OneDrive for Project Management

Project management becomes much more efficient when you integrate **OneDrive** and **SharePoint** with the other Microsoft 365 tools. These integrations provide a holistic approach to organizing, tracking, and executing your projects with a high degree of collaboration.

Project Management with SharePoint:

- **SharePoint Project Sites**: For team-based projects, SharePoint's **Team Sites** can be used to organize and centralize documents, tasks, and discussions. You can set up project-specific libraries, document repositories, calendars, and task lists all within one SharePoint site.
- **Document and Task Tracking**: As projects evolve, the need to track changes and deadlines is critical. SharePoint's **Task Lists** and **Planner integration** allow teams to stay organized and on schedule.

Project Management with OneDrive:

- **Personal Document Management for Projects**: While SharePoint is ideal for team collaboration, **OneDrive** can be used to store personal project-related documents that you're working on. You can then share them with your team when necessary.
- **Collaborating on Project Files**: Even when managing personal tasks, OneDrive allows you to collaborate on project files with your team, helping keep everything aligned.

Tracking Progress and Team Communication:

- **Using Microsoft Teams for Communication**: Teams acts as your communication hub for ongoing projects. SharePoint and OneDrive work closely with Teams, so your documents and project files are easily accessible from within the Teams interface.

- **Project Updates and Notifications**: With Teams and Planner integrated, you can receive automatic notifications about project deadlines, document updates, and task progress. This ensures everyone is aligned and can track the project's success in real time.

Part IV: Advanced Tips and Best Practices

Chapter 22: Managing Storage and Data

In this chapter, we will discuss essential strategies for **managing storage** and optimizing data organization in **OneDrive** and **SharePoint**. Proper storage management is vital for maintaining efficient workflows, minimizing data clutter, and ensuring that your cloud storage doesn't exceed its capacity. We'll cover how to monitor storage usage, clean up files, set storage limits, and follow best practices for data organization.

1. Monitoring OneDrive and SharePoint Storage Usage

Both **OneDrive** and **SharePoint** offer tools and insights that allow users to monitor their storage usage, ensuring that they don't run into capacity limits unexpectedly.

Monitoring OneDrive Storage Usage:

- **Storage Quota Overview**: OneDrive for Business typically offers 1 TB of storage per user, with the possibility of scaling to even higher limits depending on your plan. You can view your storage usage within the OneDrive settings.
  - To check storage usage, go to **OneDrive settings > Storage**.
- **Storage Usage Breakdown**: OneDrive provides a detailed breakdown of your storage usage, so you can see how much

space is taken up by **files, shared folders**, and **recycle bin** items.

- **Storage Alerts**: Set up alerts to notify you when your storage space reaches a certain percentage threshold, giving you time to act before you hit the limit.

Monitoring SharePoint Storage Usage:

- **Site Collection Storage**: Each **SharePoint site collection** has its own storage quota, which can be monitored by site administrators.
  - o To view the usage, go to the **SharePoint admin center > Sites > Active sites >** Select your site > **Storage**.
- **Storage Analytics**: SharePoint provides a **storage metrics report** that shows the size of your document libraries, as well as other data about your SharePoint environment.
- **Shared Storage**: Keep track of shared documents and files, as large files or excess versions may be consuming space across the organization.

2. Cleaning Up Files and Folders to Save Space

Managing and cleaning up data is critical for freeing up space and keeping your storage efficient. Both **OneDrive** and **SharePoint** offer options to clean up unnecessary files, manage versions, and avoid unnecessary storage usage.

Cleaning Up OneDrive:

- **Removing Old or Unnecessary Files**: Regularly review your OneDrive storage and delete files that are no longer needed. Utilize the **Search** function to find and remove old documents.
  - o Use the **OneDrive Recycle Bin** to recover files you may have accidentally deleted.
- **Emptying the Recycle Bin**: The Recycle Bin in OneDrive can store deleted files for up to 30 days before they are permanently deleted. Be sure to regularly empty the Recycle Bin to reclaim storage.
- **Managing Large Files**: Sort your files by size to find and remove large files taking up unnecessary space.

Cleaning Up SharePoint:

- **Archiving and Deleting Old Files**: SharePoint allows you to archive old project files and delete outdated documents that no longer serve a purpose. Make sure that only essential content remains in your active libraries.
- **Versioning and Document Retention Policies**: SharePoint maintains version history for documents, which can consume a significant amount of storage. Set up **versioning settings** to limit how many versions are kept or to delete older versions after a certain time.
  - o You can do this by going to **Library Settings > Versioning Settings** and selecting the appropriate retention rules.

- **Purging Old Data**: Periodically review old data stored in SharePoint libraries and use retention policies to automatically delete files based on age or usage patterns.

3. Setting Storage Limits and Quotas in SharePoint

To ensure that your SharePoint environment remains optimized and efficient, setting **storage limits and quotas** is essential, especially for larger organizations or teams with a large volume of documents.

Setting SharePoint Site Storage Limits:

- **Setting Storage Quotas**: In SharePoint, site collections have storage quotas that can be set to ensure no individual site exceeds its designated storage limits.
  - From the **SharePoint Admin Center**, navigate to **Sites > Active Sites**, select the site you want to configure, and set the **storage quota**.
- **Monitoring and Adjusting Storage**: Regularly monitor the storage usage of your SharePoint site collections. When a site collection approaches its storage quota, administrators can adjust the limits or add additional space if needed.

Quota Management:

- **Managing Storage Across Multiple Sites**: SharePoint allows you to assign storage quotas per site collection. Keep an eye on overall storage across your entire SharePoint environment to ensure fair usage and avoid unexpected performance issues.

- **Enabling Alerts for Quota Exceedance**: Configure **email notifications** to alert administrators when a site collection is nearing its storage quota or exceeding it, providing proactive warnings.

4. Best Practices for File Organization and Management

Efficient file organization is crucial for maximizing storage and ensuring that files are easy to find and access. Here are some **best practices** for organizing your files in **OneDrive** and **SharePoint**:

Best Practices for OneDrive:

- **Use Folders to Organize Files**: Create a **folder structure** in OneDrive that mirrors your workflow or project organization. Use logical and easy-to-understand naming conventions for your folders and files.
- **Regularly Sync and Clean**: Sync important files for offline access, but periodically clean your **local sync folder** to avoid storing outdated files.
- **Avoid Duplicates**: Use the **file versioning** feature to keep track of changes, rather than saving multiple copies of the same file with different names.

Best Practices for SharePoint:

- **Organize Documents in Libraries**: Create document libraries for different departments, projects, or document types. This structure keeps content organized and easy to access.

- **Leverage Metadata**: Use **metadata** (tags and custom columns) to categorize documents. This helps with searching, filtering, and organizing content beyond folder structure.
- **Implement Document Retention Policies**: Implement **retention policies** for documents to automatically delete or archive content after a set period, reducing manual cleanup efforts and keeping your storage usage efficient.
- **Version Control**: Manage **versioning settings** so only a limited number of older versions are kept for each document. This reduces unnecessary storage consumption from older versions of files.

Chapter 23: Security and Compliance

I n this chapter, we'll explore the vital aspects of **securing your files** and ensuring **compliance** within **OneDrive** and **SharePoint**. With increasing concerns over data breaches and privacy regulations, it's essential to protect your documents and sensitive data. We'll cover security measures like **encryption**, the role of **multi-factor authentication (MFA)**, and the specific **security and compliance** tools available in SharePoint. Understanding these tools will help ensure that your organization's data remains protected and compliant with legal standards.

1. Securing Your Files and Documents in OneDrive and SharePoint

Both **OneDrive** and **SharePoint** offer robust security features to safeguard your files. From file-level permissions to advanced data protection features, ensuring security is paramount.

OneDrive Security Features:

- **File-Level Permissions**: You can set **permissions** for each file or folder, allowing you to control who can view, edit, or share your documents. You can choose to share files with specific users, or with broader groups, while limiting what they can do.

- **Sharing Restrictions**: OneDrive offers the ability to limit file sharing, such as disabling the ability to share with external users or setting expiration dates for shared links.
- **Password-Protected Links**: For added security, you can create **password-protected links** for shared files, requiring recipients to enter a password to access the content.

SharePoint Security Features:

- **Granular Permissions**: SharePoint provides advanced security controls with **item-level permissions**. You can grant or restrict access to specific files, folders, or libraries based on roles and security groups.
- **Access Control**: SharePoint allows you to control who has access to different **site collections**, ensuring that sensitive content is restricted to authorized individuals only.
- **Audit Logs**: SharePoint's **audit logs** allow you to track activities on files and sites, providing transparency into who accessed or modified your documents.

2. Understanding Encryption and Data Privacy

Encryption and data privacy are essential components of any security strategy, ensuring that your data is protected both in transit and at rest.

Encryption in OneDrive and SharePoint:

- **Data in Transit**: Both **OneDrive** and **SharePoint** encrypt data in transit using **SSL (Secure Sockets Layer)**, which protects the data as it moves between your device and

Microsoft's servers. This ensures that your files remain secure during transfers.

- **Data at Rest**: Data stored in **OneDrive** and **SharePoint** is encrypted at rest using **AES-256** encryption. This ensures that even if someone gains unauthorized access to the storage systems, the data will be unreadable without the proper encryption keys.
- **End-to-End Encryption**: For certain files and scenarios, you can enable **end-to-end encryption**, which adds another layer of security by ensuring that only authorized individuals can decrypt and view the data.

Data Privacy Considerations:

- **Personal Data Protection**: With strict **GDPR (General Data Protection Regulation)** and other privacy laws in place, it is critical to ensure that personal data is handled properly. Both **OneDrive** and **SharePoint** are designed to help organizations comply with these regulations.
- **Data Loss Prevention (DLP)**: OneDrive and SharePoint offer **DLP** features, which help prevent the accidental sharing of sensitive information like credit card numbers, social security numbers, or health information.
- **Customer Data Control**: Microsoft's cloud services, including OneDrive and SharePoint, offer transparency and control over customer data, enabling organizations to manage where data is stored and how it's processed.

3. Setting Up Multi-Factor Authentication (MFA)

Multi-factor authentication (MFA) is a key security measure to ensure that only authorized users can access your OneDrive and SharePoint data. It provides an extra layer of protection beyond the usual username and password login.

What is MFA?:

MFA requires users to provide more than one form of identification before granting access. This typically involves something the user knows (password), something the user has (a smartphone or security token), or something the user is (fingerprint or facial recognition).

Setting Up MFA for OneDrive and SharePoint:

- **Enabling MFA in Microsoft 365**: Admins can enable MFA for **OneDrive** and **SharePoint** through the **Microsoft 365 admin center**. Once enabled, users will be prompted to verify their identity using a second method, such as a text message, phone call, or authentication app.
    - Navigate to the **Microsoft 365 admin center > Active users > Multi-factor authentication settings**.
- **App-Based Authentication**: One of the most common MFA methods is using an **authentication app** like **Microsoft Authenticator**, which provides secure and easy-to-use two-factor authentication.

- **MFA Best Practices**: Enforce MFA for all users, especially those accessing sensitive data. It's also recommended to use app-based authentication for a more seamless experience.

4. SharePoint's Security and Compliance Features

SharePoint includes a comprehensive suite of **security** and **compliance** features designed to help organizations manage and safeguard their data.

Compliance Center:

- The **Microsoft 365 Compliance Center** allows organizations to manage compliance across multiple Microsoft services, including **OneDrive** and **SharePoint**. It provides tools for data governance, risk management, and compliance with global privacy laws.
  - Key features include **retention policies, insider risk management, audit log search**, and **supervision policies**.

Data Loss Prevention (DLP) in SharePoint:

- DLP policies in **SharePoint** help prevent sensitive information from being shared or accessed inappropriately. You can create DLP rules to automatically detect and block the sharing of personally identifiable information (PII), financial data, or other confidential content.
  - Go to the **Security & Compliance Center > Data Loss Prevention > Create a policy**.

Retention Policies:

- **Retention policies** in SharePoint help you ensure that data is kept for the appropriate length of time for legal or regulatory reasons. Once retention policies are configured, SharePoint automatically retains, deletes, or moves data based on the rules you set.
  - o This helps protect organizations from potential legal liabilities by ensuring that data is not kept longer than necessary.

Advanced Threat Protection (ATP):

- **ATP** is available for SharePoint and OneDrive to protect against **malicious files** and threats. ATP scans files for potential risks such as malware, ransomware, and phishing attempts.
- With ATP, any files uploaded to SharePoint or OneDrive are automatically scanned for threats, helping protect your organization from malicious content.

Chapter 24: Troubleshooting Common Issues

I n this chapter, we'll address some of the most common problems users encounter while working with **OneDrive** and **SharePoint**. Whether it's syncing issues in OneDrive, permission errors in SharePoint, or file upload problems, knowing how to troubleshoot these issues will help you maintain a smooth experience. We'll walk through practical solutions for the following issues and give you tools to resolve them effectively.

1. Solving Sync Problems in OneDrive

Syncing issues are one of the most frequent problems encountered by OneDrive users. When files fail to sync properly, it can cause confusion and disrupt workflow. Here's how to troubleshoot and fix common syncing problems in OneDrive:

Possible Causes of Syncing Issues:

- **Insufficient Storage Space**: If you're running low on storage, OneDrive may not sync new or modified files.
- **Slow Internet Connection**: A poor or intermittent connection can prevent OneDrive from syncing files correctly.
- **Conflicting File Names**: Certain characters in file names (e.g., slashes, asterisks) may cause syncing errors.

- **Outdated OneDrive Client**: Using an outdated version of the OneDrive app can also lead to syncing issues.

Solutions:

- **Check Storage Space**: Ensure you have enough space in your **OneDrive** account. You can view your available storage in the **OneDrive app** or online.
- **Verify Your Internet Connection**: Ensure your internet connection is stable and fast enough for syncing. Try moving to a different network if the current one is slow.
- **Fix File Name Issues**: Look for any files with special characters or overly long file paths and rename them to standardize them.
- **Update the OneDrive Client**: Ensure that you're using the latest version of the OneDrive app. Update the app through the **Microsoft Store** or the OneDrive settings menu.

Other Fixes:

- **Pause and Resume Syncing**: Open the OneDrive app, right-click on the icon in the system tray, and select "Pause syncing." After a few minutes, resume syncing to reset the process.
- **Reset OneDrive**: If the above solutions don't work, you can try resetting the OneDrive client. This will not delete any files, but it will reset syncing to its default state.

2. Dealing with Permission Errors in SharePoint

One of the most common issues in SharePoint is encountering **permission errors** when trying to access files or document libraries. This can happen when you lack the necessary access or when permissions are misconfigured.

Possible Causes of Permission Issues:

- **Lack of Proper Permissions**: If you don't have the right permissions, you may not be able to view, edit, or share a file.
- **Inherited Permissions**: SharePoint permissions can be inherited from parent sites, and sometimes these inherited permissions may block you from accessing content.
- **Role Misconfiguration**: If a user is not assigned the correct SharePoint role, it may cause permission errors.

Solutions:

- **Check Your Permissions**: Ask the site owner or administrator to confirm that you have the correct permissions to access the site or document library. You can also check permissions yourself by navigating to the **site settings** and reviewing your **user permissions**.
- **Request Access**: If you encounter a permission error, you may be able to request access directly through SharePoint's "Request Access" feature. This will send a request to the site owner or administrator.
- **Stop Inheriting Permissions**: If the issue is caused by inherited permissions, ask the site owner to **stop inheriting**

permissions for the library or list in question. They can then assign permissions manually.

3. Fixing Common File Upload Problems

File upload issues can occur for several reasons, from file size limits to network errors. Here's how to troubleshoot file upload problems in OneDrive and SharePoint.

Possible Causes of Upload Problems:

- **File Size Limitations**: OneDrive and SharePoint both have file size limits, and exceeding these limits can result in upload failure.
- **File Type Restrictions**: Certain file types may be blocked for security reasons.
- **Network Interruptions**: A poor or disconnected internet connection can cause file uploads to fail.
- **File Corruption**: Sometimes, the file being uploaded may be corrupted or incomplete, which will prevent it from being uploaded successfully.

Solutions:

- **Check File Size Limits**: Ensure your file does not exceed OneDrive's or SharePoint's **file size limit**. For **OneDrive**, the limit is usually **100GB** per file (depending on your plan), while SharePoint allows up to **15GB** per file. You may need to compress large files or split them into smaller parts.
- **Check File Types**: Ensure that the file you're trying to upload is not blocked by SharePoint's or OneDrive's **file type**

restrictions. You can find this list in the **SharePoint settings** or **OneDrive admin settings**.

- **Upload with a Stable Connection**: Try uploading files when you have a stable internet connection. You can also attempt the upload in **smaller batches** to ensure each file uploads successfully.
- **Try a Different Method**: If the web upload is not working, you can try using the **OneDrive desktop app** or **SharePoint Sync** to upload files.

4. Resolving Conflicts in Document Libraries

Document libraries in **SharePoint** and **OneDrive** can sometimes encounter **file conflicts**. This happens when multiple people try to edit the same file at the same time, or if a file was updated on multiple devices without syncing properly.

Possible Causes of File Conflicts:

- **Simultaneous Edits**: If multiple users are editing the same document at once, it can cause versioning issues or conflicts.
- **Outdated Sync**: When one user updates a file offline and then another user makes changes online, a conflict can occur when the files sync.
- **File Locking Issues**: SharePoint and OneDrive use **file locking** to prevent conflicts, but sometimes the lock can expire or be mismanaged.

Solutions:

- **Use Version History**: OneDrive and SharePoint both have a **version history** feature. If a conflict arises, use this feature to restore an earlier version of the file. Right-click the file and select **Version History** to view and restore past versions.
- **Resolve Conflicting Copies**: If a conflict is detected, you'll be given the option to **merge changes** or keep the two versions as separate files. Choose the appropriate action based on the changes made.
- **Ensure Proper Syncing**: Make sure that all users are syncing their changes properly before working on the file again. Always sync files to the cloud after making changes.

Part V: Real-Life Use Cases and Scenarios

Chapter 25: Personal Use of OneDrive and SharePoint

In this chapter, we will explore how to leverage **OneDrive** and **SharePoint** for personal use. These powerful tools, typically associated with business and team collaboration, can also be used effectively for personal file storage, backup, and managing personal projects. By the end of this chapter, you will understand how to organize, store, and collaborate on your personal files using both OneDrive and SharePoint.

1. Using OneDrive for Personal File Storage and Backup

OneDrive is an excellent cloud-based storage solution for individuals looking to store, back up, and access personal files from any device. It's simple to use, and with a free or paid OneDrive plan, you can ensure your documents, photos, and important files are safely stored and always accessible.

Key Features for Personal Use:

- **Cloud Storage**: OneDrive provides cloud storage that allows you to store a variety of file types, from documents and spreadsheets to photos and videos. It's especially useful for keeping files safe and easily accessible without occupying your device's storage space.

- **Automatic Backup**: OneDrive can automatically back up files and folders from your device. You can choose specific folders (like **Documents**, **Pictures**, and **Desktop**) to sync and back up, ensuring your important files are protected.
- **Access from Anywhere**: As long as you have an internet connection, you can access your files from any device using the OneDrive mobile app, website, or desktop app. This gives you flexibility, whether you're at home, traveling, or at work.

How to Use OneDrive for Personal File Storage:

- **Upload Files**: Simply drag and drop files into the OneDrive folder on your computer or upload them through the OneDrive web interface. You can also organize your files by creating folders to group them into categories.
- **Sync Your Files**: Install the OneDrive desktop app to sync files across your devices. Once synced, any changes made to a file will automatically update across all devices linked to your OneDrive account.
- **Back Up Your Files**: Enable automatic backup for key folders like **Documents** and **Photos** to ensure your important files are always backed up to the cloud. You can adjust backup settings in the **OneDrive settings** menu on your device.

2. Organizing Photos and Videos in OneDrive

For personal users who want to store and organize their photos and videos, OneDrive is an ideal solution. It offers **automatic photo upload, photo organization tools**, and **search features** that make it easy to manage media files.

Organizing Photos in OneDrive:

- **Photo Folders**: Create specific folders to organize your photos into categories such as "Vacation," "Family," or "Work Projects." This will help you keep your files easily accessible.
- **Automatic Upload**: You can set up **auto-upload** from your phone or camera to OneDrive. Whenever you capture new photos or videos, they'll be automatically uploaded to OneDrive, freeing up space on your device.
- **Create Albums**: OneDrive allows you to organize photos into **albums** that can be shared with family and friends. You can create albums by year, event, or any other categorization that makes sense to you.
- **Photo and Video Editing**: OneDrive integrates with **Microsoft Photos**, which lets you view, edit, and organize photos directly in the cloud. You can rotate, crop, adjust lighting, and even create albums or slideshows for sharing.

Using OneDrive's Search Features:

- OneDrive uses **AI-powered search** to help you quickly find photos and videos. You can search by date, file name, or even content in the image itself (such as objects, places, or text in your photos).
- You can also tag your photos with specific labels or descriptions, making them easier to find later on.

3. SharePoint for Personal Projects and Collaboration

While SharePoint is primarily designed for business and team use, it also offers features that can be highly beneficial for personal projects and collaboration. Whether you are working on a solo project or collaborating with friends or family, SharePoint can serve as an effective tool for organizing and sharing information.

Using SharePoint for Personal Projects:

- **Creating a Personal SharePoint Site**: You can create a personal **SharePoint site** to manage and organize your personal projects. Whether it's a travel plan, a DIY project, or a creative writing project, SharePoint allows you to keep all related documents, tasks, and notes in one place.
- **Document Management**: SharePoint's **document libraries** allow you to store and organize all your project-related files. You can create custom views and organize documents using metadata for better management.
- **Using Lists for Project Management**: SharePoint **lists** are perfect for keeping track of tasks, deadlines, and other project-related data. For example, you can create a list to manage shopping lists, project tasks, or inventory for your personal project.

Collaborating in SharePoint:

- **Sharing with Family and Friends**: SharePoint lets you share documents and folders with others, making it ideal for collaborative personal projects. You can give collaborators view, edit, or full access to content.

- **Document Co-authoring**: When working on a document or spreadsheet with others, SharePoint allows real-time collaboration where multiple users can work on the document simultaneously. This is ideal for group projects, whether they're work-related or personal.
- **Creating Personal Team Sites**: If you're working on a personal project with a group of people (such as planning a family event, organizing a community project, or collaborating on creative work), you can create a **Team Site** in SharePoint to bring everyone together. A SharePoint Team Site offers a central place to share documents, calendars, and communication tools.

Benefits of Using OneDrive and SharePoint for Personal Use

OneDrive for Personal Use:

- **Backup and Recovery**: OneDrive offers **version history** and the ability to recover deleted files, making it a reliable option for keeping personal files safe.
- **Access from Any Device**: You can access your personal files on OneDrive from virtually any device, whether it's your smartphone, tablet, or desktop.
- **Sharing**: OneDrive allows you to share files and folders with anyone, even if they don't have a Microsoft account, making it easy to collaborate on personal projects.

SharePoint for Personal Use:

- **Project Management Tools**: SharePoint's integration with **Microsoft Teams** and **Planner** can be used to manage and communicate effectively within personal project teams.
- **Customization**: You can customize SharePoint sites to fit your personal needs, whether it's organizing a home renovation project, planning a trip, or sharing creative work with collaborators.
- **Security and Control**: SharePoint offers advanced security features, which can help you control who has access to your personal data. You can restrict access to sensitive project information while collaborating with others.

Chapter 26: Small Business Use

In this chapter, we will focus on how **OneDrive** and **SharePoint** can be utilized by small businesses to improve collaboration, streamline document management, and ensure efficient file sharing. With small teams often needing flexible, affordable solutions to manage business documents, both of these tools offer essential features that support growth and productivity. By the end of this chapter, you'll have a solid understanding of how to set up, manage, and collaborate with your team using these platforms.

1. Setting Up OneDrive and SharePoint for Small Teams

When setting up OneDrive and SharePoint for a small business or team, it's important to understand how both platforms work together while offering distinct features that cater to different needs. OneDrive serves as a personal storage solution, while SharePoint excels in team collaboration, document management, and centralized communication.

Getting Started with OneDrive:

- **Create Business Accounts**: Small businesses can take advantage of **Microsoft 365 Business** subscriptions to get OneDrive and SharePoint. When you set up OneDrive for business, each team member will receive their own

OneDrive account with cloud storage that is accessible from anywhere.

- **Assigning Storage**: OneDrive for business provides 1 TB of storage per user, which can be upgraded as the company grows. As the administrator, you can manage storage and ensure each team member has access to the appropriate amount.

- **Syncing Files**: Encourage team members to sync important business files to their local devices using the **OneDrive desktop app**. This way, employees can access files offline and have them updated automatically when connected to the internet.

Setting Up SharePoint:

- **Create a SharePoint Site**: SharePoint provides a centralized location for storing documents and information. To set it up for your small business:
  1. **Create a SharePoint Site**: You can create **Team Sites** for different departments or projects (e.g., marketing, sales, finance). Each site has a **document library** where files are stored.
  2. **Set Permissions**: Control access by setting permissions for each team member based on their roles. For example, you may give your marketing team full access to the marketing site, while only allowing read-only access for others.
  3. **Customize Your Site**: Tailor the look and structure of the SharePoint site by adding libraries, lists, and links to important resources, making it easier for

your team to access necessary documents and information.

2. Collaborative Document Management for Small Businesses

One of the key benefits of OneDrive and SharePoint is their ability to facilitate **real-time collaboration** on documents, making them essential tools for small businesses. Instead of sending documents back and forth, your team can work together on a document in real time, whether they are working remotely or in the same office.

Collaborating with OneDrive:

- **Sharing Files and Folders**: You can easily share files and folders in OneDrive with your team by creating a shared folder and giving team members either **view or edit access**.
- **Co-authoring**: With **co-authoring**, multiple team members can edit the same document at the same time without worrying about version conflicts. OneDrive integrates with **Microsoft Office apps** like Word, Excel, and PowerPoint to allow real-time updates and feedback.
- **Commenting and Marking Changes**: Team members can leave comments directly in the documents. OneDrive supports the **Track Changes** feature, so you can see what edits have been made and by whom.

Collaborating with SharePoint:

- **Document Libraries**: SharePoint's **document libraries** allow multiple users to upload, organize, and work on documents together. You can share entire libraries or specific files and assign permissions to control who can access or edit the content.

- **Version Control**: SharePoint automatically maintains **version history**, so you can view and restore previous versions of documents. This is helpful for tracking changes or recovering files after mistakes.
- **Approval Workflows**: SharePoint can also automate document workflows. For example, you can create an approval process that requires a document to be approved by a team member before it's published or finalized.
- **Alerts and Notifications**: Set up **alerts** to notify team members when files or folders are modified, ensuring that everyone stays informed about changes to important business documents.

3. Best Practices for Team Collaboration and File Sharing

Effective collaboration and efficient file sharing are essential for small businesses to function smoothly. By using **OneDrive** and **SharePoint** in the right ways, you can improve productivity, ensure document security, and streamline team workflows.

Best Practices for Using OneDrive and SharePoint:

- **Standardize File Organization**: Create clear, consistent naming conventions and folder structures for business documents. This will help team members find files quickly and avoid confusion over file versions.

- **Centralize Important Documents**: Store important company-wide documents (e.g., policies, financial reports, contracts) on **SharePoint** so they can be easily accessed by the team. Use OneDrive for more personal or individual documents that don't need to be shared with the team.

- **Use Microsoft Teams for Communication**: For efficient communication alongside document collaboration, integrate **OneDrive** and **SharePoint** with **Microsoft Teams**. Teams allows for messaging, video calls, and document sharing in real time, keeping everyone on the same page.

- **Backup Critical Documents**: Regularly back up critical business documents to **OneDrive** and **SharePoint** to ensure data is safe in case of accidental deletion or technical issues. Both platforms automatically back up files in the cloud, reducing the risk of data loss.

- **Create Task Lists in SharePoint**: Use **SharePoint lists** to create task lists or project management boards. You can track the progress of team projects, assign tasks, set deadlines, and monitor status updates, all within SharePoint.

- **Collaborate Safely with External Partners**: Both **OneDrive** and **SharePoint** allow you to share files with external collaborators securely. Ensure you set permissions for external users to only access the necessary files and have read-only access when appropriate.

Tips for Secure File Sharing:

- **Set Permissions**: Be sure to define who can access, edit, or share documents. Use **SharePoint permissions** to control access at a granular level, while OneDrive allows you to manage sharing and permissions on individual files.

- **Enable Multi-Factor Authentication (MFA)**: For added security, enable **MFA** for all users. This ensures that even if someone's password is compromised, the account remains protected.
- **Use Document Expiration Dates**: If you share files with external partners, set **expiration dates** for access to ensure that the shared file is only accessible for a specific period.

Chapter 27: Corporate and Enterprise Use

This chapter explores how **OneDrive** and **SharePoint** can meet the demands of large organizations and enterprises. From enterprise-level file management and advanced permissions to robust security and storage solutions, these tools are designed to handle the complexities of large-scale collaboration while ensuring data integrity and security.

1. Enterprise-Level File Management with SharePoint

SharePoint is an ideal platform for enterprise-level file management, offering tools to organize, store, and manage vast amounts of data efficiently. For corporations dealing with thousands of files across multiple departments, SharePoint's scalability and advanced management features are essential.

Key Features for Enterprise File Management:

- **Centralized Document Libraries**: SharePoint allows enterprises to create centralized repositories for files, enabling employees across departments to access essential documents. For example:
    - HR documents (policies, guidelines).
    - Marketing materials (campaigns, assets).
    - Legal documents (contracts, compliance files).

- **Metadata Tagging and Classification**: Use metadata tags to classify files by categories such as department, project, or sensitivity level. This simplifies searching and ensures employees can quickly locate the files they need.
- **Version Control and History**: SharePoint maintains detailed version histories of all files, enabling employees to review previous versions, restore older files, or track changes over time.
- **Content Types and Templates**: Enterprises can create standardized content types and document templates to ensure consistency in file formatting and structure across departments.

Document Retention Policies:

- SharePoint supports automated **retention policies** that comply with legal and regulatory requirements, ensuring that files are archived or deleted based on predefined rules.

2. Managing Teams and Permissions in SharePoint for Large Organizations

In large organizations, managing users, teams, and permissions is critical to maintaining security and efficiency. SharePoint offers robust tools to structure teams, assign roles, and control access to sensitive information.

Organizing Teams and Sites:

- **Team Sites**: Create dedicated sites for each department, project, or team. For example:

- A **Sales Team Site** for sharing sales reports and CRM data.
- A **Product Development Site** for collaborating on new designs and innovations.
- A **Board Members' Site** for confidential executive discussions and documents.
- **Hub Sites**: Use hub sites to connect related team sites across the organization, creating a unified hierarchy that simplifies navigation and search.

Managing Permissions:

- **Granular Permissions**: SharePoint allows you to assign permissions at the site, library, folder, or document level. For example:
  - HR can restrict sensitive employee data to specific managers.
  - Finance can limit budget documents to senior executives.
- **Role-Based Access Control (RBAC)**: Assign predefined roles like **Site Owners**, **Members**, and **Visitors** to streamline permissions management.
- **Group-Based Permissions**: Integrate SharePoint with **Microsoft 365 Groups** to manage permissions efficiently across platforms (e.g., SharePoint, Teams, Planner).

Monitoring and Auditing:

- SharePoint's **audit logs** provide insights into user activities, helping administrators monitor file access, edits, and sharing activities. This is especially important for identifying and mitigating potential security risks.

3. Enterprise-Level Storage and Security Management

Enterprises require robust storage and security features to handle large volumes of data and protect sensitive information. SharePoint and OneDrive are equipped with advanced tools to meet these needs.

Storage Solutions:

- **Scalable Storage**: Enterprises can take advantage of scalable storage plans, allowing organizations to expand storage capacity as their data needs grow.
- **SharePoint Document Libraries**: Each library can store up to **30 million items**, making it suitable for enterprise-scale file management.
- **OneDrive Storage for Employees**: Each employee account includes **1 TB of OneDrive storage** by default, with options to increase as needed.

Security Features:

- **Data Encryption**:
  - Files stored in OneDrive and SharePoint are encrypted at rest and in transit, ensuring that sensitive information is protected from unauthorized access.

- o Microsoft uses **Advanced Encryption Standard (AES-256)** to secure data.
- **Multi-Factor Authentication (MFA)**:
  - o Enable MFA for all users to add an extra layer of security. This ensures that even if passwords are compromised, unauthorized access is prevented.
- **Conditional Access Policies**:
  - o Use conditional access policies to restrict access based on criteria like location, device, or role. For instance, block access to sensitive files from unknown or unsecured devices.
- **Data Loss Prevention (DLP)**:
  - o SharePoint and OneDrive support **DLP policies** that help prevent accidental sharing of confidential information. DLP can automatically flag or block files containing sensitive data such as credit card numbers or personally identifiable information (PII).
- **Ransomware Recovery**:
  - o Both platforms offer built-in tools to detect ransomware attacks and recover affected files.

Compliance Management:

- **Regulatory Compliance**:
  - o SharePoint is designed to meet various compliance standards, including **GDPR, HIPAA**, and **ISO 27001**. Administrators can configure compliance settings to meet industry-specific requirements.
- **Retention Labels and Policies**:

- Apply retention labels to documents to ensure that they are retained or deleted according to organizational or legal policies.

Index

Advanced Threat Protection
  (ATP):, 191
Alerts, 141
Auto-Save and Backup, 86
Check In/Check Out, 123
Cloud Storage, 9
Co-authoring, 166
Co-Authoring, 79
Collaboration, 77
Comments, 81
Comments:, 140
Communication Sites, 99
Compliance Center, 190
Data Loss Prevention (DLP),
  190
Document Libraries, 113
File Recovery, 72
File Sharing, 11
File Syncing, 10
Groups and Roles, 133
InfoPath, 157
Lists, 115
Managing Notifications, 85
means, *i*

Metadata, 122
Microsoft Account, 16
Microsoft Teams Integration,
  173
Multi-Factor Authentication
  (MFA), 189
Notifications:, 143
Offline Access, 62, 171
OneDrive, 8
OneDrive Dashboard, 29
OneDrive Interface, 24
OneDrive Sync, 59
Permission Levels, 128
Permissions, 51
Power Automate, 151
Public Links, 55
Real-Time Edits, 78
Recycle Bin, 43
Restoring Previous Versions,
  71
Retention Policies, 191
Share, 46
Shared Links, 54
SharePoint, 96

SharePoint Account, 102
SharePoint Interface, 111
SharePoint Lists, 144
SharePoint Security Groups, 129
SharePoint Site, 103
SharePoint View, 117
Sharing Files, 11
Sharing with Specific People, 55
Storage Limits and Quotas, 183

Storage Space, 88
Storage Usage, 180
Subfolders, 39
Syncing Issues, 66
Team Sites, 98
Templates, 153
Track Changes, 81
Upload, 35
Uploading Documents, 119
Version History, 12, 68
Workflows, 150

www.ingramcontent.com/pod-product-compliance
Lightning Source LLC
LaVergne TN
LVHW051733050326
832903LV00023B/899